Praise for *Love Your Body, Love Your Life*

"Read this book and you will discover that there is only one beauty, and you are that."

—Deepak Chopra

"In traditional cultures, the most powerful healers are those who have learned to heal themselves. Sarah Maria's personal journey to loving her body and her life offers a proven path for those seeking a healthy, conscious relationship with their bodies."

—David Simon, MD, the Chopra Center for Well-Being

"There are countless women and men who suffer unnecessarily because they don't like their looks. Sarah Maria reveals that there is a way to feel great no matter what, and she offers powerful tools to help you feel beautiful regardless of your current shape or size. Read this book and you will begin to love your body."

—Marci Shimoff, *New York Times* bestselling author of *Happy for No Reason* and featured teacher in *The Secret*

"Sarah Maria has created a most practical, step-by-step journey for healing Negative Body Obsession. Following these steps awakens the inner healer in the heart of the reader and truly unfolds the inner treasures of joy, love and bliss."

—Vasant Lad, BAMS, MASc, Ayurvedic Physician, the Ayurvedic Institute, Albuquerque, NM

"Powerful, honest, and elegantly written. An amazing concept that goes beyond the idea of self-love and taps into the notion that one's love equals one's peace."

—Ira M. Sacker, MD, eating disorders specialist, international expert for more than thirty-five years, and bestselling author of *Dying to Be Thin* and *Regaining Your Self*

"Congratulations to Sarah Maria for creating this valuable gift for both women and men and those who cherish them. This clear and reliable process for reclaiming the value and beauty of our bodies makes *Love Your Body, Love Your Life* a must-read."

—Kathlyn Hendricks, PhD, ADTR, Director of Training, The Hendricks Institute, bestselling author of *Conscious Loving*

"*Love Your Body, Love Your Life* is a book written from the heart by a gifted author who has stepped into the transformational fire of learning to love herself and her body. Rich with life-changing information, each word charged with genuine compassion, this book provides the guidance, the hope, and the courage to let go of distorted perceptions that prevent you from loving your body. As a medical intuitive, I have witnessed the miracle of creating the health and the life one desires by merely learning to love oneself. I highly recommend this exceptional book. Job well done, Sarah Maria."

—Carol Ritberger, PhD, author of *Healing Happens with Your Help . . . Uncovering the Hidden Meanings Behind Illness*

"As a psychotherapist in practice for over thirty years, I have listened to the suffering of women and now often men as they struggle with images of body image and beauty. Self-esteem is hitched to this struggle and brings forth a compounding of problems in an effort to find solutions. Sarah Maria has provided a clear, concise, step-by-step formula to assist people in breaking free from patterns of thought and behavior that keep them trapped. She offers a vision of healing that has the potential for life transformation, and inner peace. This book is an important contribution to breaking the cycle of body image struggles."

—JoAnn A. DePetro, MA, MFT, Director, Center for Family Solutions

"It is well known that you attract what you think about. Your outer reality is a direct reflection of how you feel about yourself. When you feel that you are not thin enough, young enough, beautiful enough, or not enough, period, your life reflects this sense of lack and insecurity. On the other hand, when you recognize that you are, at your essence, beautiful, valuable, worthy, and wonderful, your life will begin to reflect this abundance and greatness. Sarah Maria's step-by-step method will show you how to recognize your true beauty so you can create the life of your dreams."

—Christy Whitman, bestselling author, Certified Law of Attraction Coach, and founder of www.7essentiallaws.com

"As a healer, I know that my patients' thoughts have the ability to determine their health or lack of it. Sarah Maria's step-by-step program will give you the tools you need to break free from negative thoughts, beliefs, and behaviors so that you can claim the health and the life you deserve. Sarah Maria shows you how to discover your unique, radiant, glorious beauty so that you can truly love your body and love your life. You can live a life of health, peace, joy, and abundance, and this book will show you how!"

—Dr. Darren Weissman, author of The Power of Infinite Love and Gratitude

"Life is a journey to discover our own unconditional self-love because only when you truly learn to love yourself will you have the ability to love others. In Love Your Body, Love Your Life, Sarah Maria gives the reader a wonderful five-step process to help you overcome Negative Body Obsession and create a life that you love. You'll love this book and you'll love Sarah Maria for writing it."

—Kurek Ashley, international bestselling author of *How Would Love Respond?*

"Contrary to popular belief, both men and women go through periods of their lives when they don't feel good enough. As long as insecurity, doubt, and shame are a part of your internal conversation, you will suffer. Period. By using the easy-to-follow steps and tools outlined in this amazing book, you will break this unnecessary pattern and find true freedom and joy."

—Max Simon, founder of **self**centered, *www.getselfcentered.com*

"With humor, insight, and true compassion, Sarah Maria invites the reader to journey toward their healing through the pain of their own experience. She subtly challenges their biggest fear of 'If you take away my negative body obsession, who will I be?' and offers a tangible journey to reconnect them with their true purpose. A wonderful mix of honoring the reader's predicament, opening them up to their spiritual essence, and integrating practical ways to embody the change that the reader is doubtless enticed into desiring. Thus, the reader's pain is transformed into a creative means of providing service for others."

—Clare Mann, psychologist, author, and professional speaker, *www.PathofConsciousLeadership.com*

"If you are ready to change your life by breaking free from the negative beliefs, thoughts, and behaviors that you have about yourself, then this book is for you. I have had the honor of working one-on-one with Sarah Maria and it has been a truly transformational experience. Working with Sarah Maria has helped me to see that I am inherently lovable, beautiful, and valuable, no matter what. She has given me tools and techniques to break free from self-hatred and put love in its place. I am incredibly grateful for her and her incredible program. I recommend this book for anyone who wants to love her body and love her life."

—Gabrielle Forleo, program consultant at the Chopra Center for Well-Being

"Sarah Maria's teachings are an amazing gift. It's an outstanding program that has changed my life! I highly recommend Sarah Maria's program to anyone who wants to experience living their most successful, beautiful life."

—Mary Schmidt

"I know that anyone who reads *Love Your Body, Love Your Life* will find themselves positively transformed spiritually, physically, and mentally. Since working with Sarah, I now understand just how much power I truly have over my own life. I now know that I am not a victim of my thoughts about my body and life, but a product of them, and that I have the power to change every area of my life as I take responsibility for my thoughts and actions, and, with love and forgiveness, begin to change them. Sarah Maria's simple process for changing Negative Body Obsession has helped me become a more healthy, confident, creative, powerful woman. She helped teach me that I have the power to create anything in my life I desire. I highly recommend reading Sarah's book, and private coaching with Sarah as well."

—Barbi (Barbara Wiedle)

"I was a full-blown anorexic for years, then a serious undereater for many more. I am paying the price now with major health conditions originating with my controlling relationship with food. I always saw this as a great victory in my life. Now I realize it was anything but. I came to this realization in my work with Sarah Maria. She leads with deep wisdom and penetrating insight. She has extensive knowledge and an understanding of eating disorders that comes in part from her own personal experience. She gives me hope to see what she has overcome and accomplished. Sarah Maria has shared many tools with me. But much more important to me, and what has been most meaningful, has been her quality of compassion. It is a gift and is like a gentle, deep awakening. Sarah Maria is a remarkable individual who works with the physical, mental, emotional, and spiritual person. I cannot thank her in a way that seems adequate."

—Leigh Ann Jones

"Whether my weight is up or down or exactly where it should be, there are days when I just don't feel happy with my body. And frankly, I get exhausted from having to even think about it. Sarah Maria has helped me take a vacation from this endless, often self-destructive cycle that we are all guilty of. Her work reminds me that I am not defined by my body . . . and that it's perfectly okay to make peace with the wonderful inhabitant in my body that is the real me. In fact, once I am not in conflict with my outside, I can feel my inside relax and begin to make the changes I wish to make on a long-term basis. How precious a gift—to have someone give you the tools to love yourself. Thank you, Sarah Maria!"

—Sandy Frye, graphic designer

Love Your
Body,
Love Your
Life

5 Steps to End Negative Body Obsession
and Start Living Happily and Confidently

Sarah Maria

Avon, Massachusetts

Published by Adams Media,
a division of F+W Media, Inc.
57 Littlefield Street,
Avon, MA 02322. U.S.A.
www.adamsmedia.com

ISBN 10: 1-60550-153-0
ISBN 13: 978-1-60550-153-6

Printed in the United States of America.

J   I   H   G   F   E   D   C   B

**Library of Congress Cataloging-in-
Publication Data**
is available from the publisher.

To every woman who has ever felt that she is not beautiful enough; to every man who has ever felt that he is not strong enough:

May you discover your Beauty
May you revel in your Glory
May you uncover your Vitality
May you rejoice in your Divinity
Knowing always that at your essence
You are LOVE

Contents

ACKNOWLEDGMENTS

In writing this acknowledgment section, I kept trying to come up with something nonclichéd—something that didn't amount to "This book has been the result of help from so many people!" I couldn't. This book has been dependent on the help of so many people! Everyone who has ever entered my life has helped in the formation of this book in some way. Even you, the reader, has helped in the writing of this book. Thank you to everyone who has accompanied me on my journey for a short or for a long time. Specifically:

Thank you, Deepak Chopra and David Simon. Deepak, your writings and teachings burst into my soul and launched me on a path that has forever changed my life. Your wisdom touches me every single day. David, your honest words and beautiful presence bathed me in hope, health, and vision that transformed my existence. Your presence is an inspiration.

Thank you to Wayne Dyer for your wise teachings. Your writings have made a profound contribution to this book and to my life.

Thank you to Jack Canfield. Your Success Principles have helped catapult my self-esteem and my energy to the next level. Thank you to the Hoffman Process and my teacher Jane Biondi. Thank you to everyone at the Chopra Center. Thank you, Gabrielle Forleo, for your warmth and friendship, for being a ray of sunshine in the midst of darkness. Thank you to Davidji for your recommendation and powerful hugs.

Thank you to Jo Ann De Petro at the Center for Family Solutions. Thank you to Mark Horner. An enormous thank-you to Eric Rudney for your unwavering friendship.

Thank you to everyone who helped me take my idea and turn it into a book. Thank you to Annetta Hanna for helping me craft an incredible proposal.

A huge thank-you to John Willig, my agent—thank you for taking a chance on me. Andrea Norville, Laura Daly, and everyone at Adams Media, thank you so much for believing in me and in this project.

Shunmugakailash, your research help was invaluable. Thank you!

Thank you to Stephanie Beckstrom and Grant Day for your friendship and support. Thank you Andrea Lake for your friendship and insight.

Kris Clark—thank you so much for everything! Your enthusiasm, support, encouragement, and friendship refresh me daily.

Thank you to my family. Thank you to Jason, Keely, Tyler, Savannah, Linda, Allen, Cameron, Collette, Ronnie, Kimmy, Andrew, and Amanda for being in my life. Thank you to Nana and Pa, Aunt Jil, Uncle George, and Natalie Kate—I love you all.

For my parents:

Mom, words can never, ever express the depth and breadth of my love and gratitude for everything you have given to me. You have been there steadfastly and constantly, offering support and encouragement. Thank you for your unwavering vision in me.

Dad, you are and always have been my hero. Your clarity, vision, and leadership have shown me what is possible. You taught me to never live the mediocre, but to always strive for greatness. Thank you for your ongoing and unwavering support.

Ultimately,

Thank you, oh Universal Source
For the Greatest Blessing of Service
May I spend my life in service to You
May love radiate out purely from me
Transforming the lives of everyone I meet
May I take away the pain of the world.

INTRODUCTION

I know how you feel. I've been there.

I've hated my body. I've struggled with a love/hate relationship with food. I've dieted. I've lost weight and then gained it all back. I've starved myself; I've binged, and I've purged. I've felt sorry for myself, and then hated myself for feeling that way. I've felt guilty; I've felt ashamed. I've believed all the self-deprecating thoughts in my head.

I've told myself that if only I was thinner, I'd be happier. I've told myself that if only I control the size of my body, everything would be okay. I've told myself that I was the only person feeling this way.

Here's the amazing thing—*I don't live like that anymore*. My life has gone from pure hell to heavenly. And so can yours.

Really, it can.

Your life can be transformed from one of suffering, angst, anxiety, and misery to one of energy, happiness, love, and beauty. This book will take you from a place of insecurity and weakness to a place of confidence and strength. I'll show you how to discover that you are beautiful just as you are, right now. For years, I attempted to find peace, happiness, and success by controlling my body. I accepted the pervasive cultural myth that if I was thin, then I was beautiful. If I was beautiful, then I was worthwhile, then I was successful, then I was accomplished, then I was lovable. I made my self-worth dependent on external objects. My feeling good about myself was contingent on everything working out a certain way, which is always a precarious and tenuous position. Sound familiar?

Ultimately I came to understand that my self-worth had nothing to do with these externals. My beauty had nothing to do with the size of my body. I discovered that my self-worth is an intrinsic part of who I am. I am beautiful simply because I exist. I am lovable simply because I am. And so are you.

Amazingly, when I began to accept and love myself unconditionally, everything else in my life began to change as well. My health improved.

I began to experience joy, happiness, and love on a regular basis. I began to live a life that was fun, exciting, and filled with passion. I began to love my body and love my life.

Success, lovability, beauty, and value are not things you have to wait to achieve at some later date, when the circumstances of your life change. Experience them right now, in this moment. You are inherently beautiful; you are inherently lovable; you are inherently valuable; you are inherently worthwhile. As you begin to realize this, then the external circumstances and events in your life will begin to shift as well.

This book is for anyone who wants to gain more from life, anyone who wants to achieve a higher level of health, fitness, love, and vitality. It is for anyone who knows deep down inside there is some greatness within them waiting to be born.

Thank you for joining me on this journey. It is the highest honor to accompany you on your path to happiness and health.

This is not a book that you want to leave on your bookshelf. It is not a book that you want to scan and then forget about. This is a book that you want to read and reread. Complete the exercises (look for them on the gray-shaded pages); take advantage of the resources. When you do this, your life will begin to be transformed. You will find yourself experiencing more beauty, more love, more energy, and more vitality than you could ever imagine. You will find yourself living in a state of love and accomplishing your heart's desire. You will find yourself loving your body and loving your life.

Part I

Understanding
Your Journey

CHAPTER ONE

You Are Not Alone: Struggling with Negative Body Obsession

Have you ever looked in the mirror and been dismayed by the cellulite on your thighs or the wrinkles around your eyes? Have you thought about buying a new bathing suit but cringed at the idea of looking at yourself in the dressing room mirror? Have you ever longed to be taller, thinner, younger, or stronger?

If you answered yes to any of these questions, you are not alone. In fact, you are among the 80 to 90 percent of women, and growing number of men, who dislike their physical appearance and are dissatisfied with their bodies. Body hatred has become an epidemic of unfathomable proportions in this culture.

How does this dissatisfaction manifest itself in your life? In more ways than you might imagine. Beauty and body size are often associated with success—in romance, business, or any other facet of life, and if you don't think you meet society's "beauty ideal," you may feel inadequate, ashamed, and embarrassed. Consciously or unconsciously, you suffer unnecessarily because you don't think you are beautiful enough, thin enough, or good enough to live the life of your dreams, the life you deserve. You accept less, much less, than you truly want, need, or deserve, because you feel inadequate about your body and yourself.

The truth is that your sense of inadequacy is an illusion, or more a *delusion*. Yes, it's true. Many Americans suffer from this grand delusion: If I am not thin/tall/toned/beautiful/young enough, I can't live my life fully or realize my dreams. Rather than truly loving our bodies, minds, and souls, we want to nip and tuck, slice and dice, starve and purge our way to being adequate. We think we need to *change* something about ourselves in order to be deserving of love, attention, and affection.

What Is Negative Body Obsession?

This deluded sense of inadequacy has a name: Negative Body Obsession, or NBO. NBO is a condition marked by a near-constant critical rumination on one's appearance. Though NBO has yet to show up in the psychologist's bible *Diagnostic and Statistical Manual of Mental Disorders*, it is a very real, very prevalent, and, dare I say, nearly ubiquitous condition in modern society.

Do You Have NBO?

How do you know if you are suffering from Negative Body Obsession? No blood test will tell you; it's a matter of evaluating your feelings and reactions at certain moments. For example, Negative Body Obsession is the:

- Sigh of resignation when you notice the wrinkles around your eyes
- Grimace when your best friend gets a boob job and you wonder if you should, too
- Feeling of defeat when you realize your high school jeans no longer fit
- Panic you feel when you realize you ate too much at Thanksgiving dinner
- Anxious thought that you must maintain your physique in order to get the relationship or the job you want

NBO is any and every thought, feeling, and action that makes your sense of self-worth dependent on your physical appearance. It is the thought that implies "If I am thin, I will be beautiful." It is the outlook that says "If I didn't have these wrinkles, I would be attractive." It is the voice that says "If I lose weight, I will feel good about myself." It is the feeling that if only you were taller, thinner, younger, or stronger, you would be more deserving, more attractive, and more lovable than you are right now.

Making Improvements to Your Body for the Right Reasons

Let me address a potential point of confusion from the get-go. The problem with NBO is not that it makes you want to change, per se. There is nothing inherently wrong with wanting to get stronger; to become healthier; and to feel more radiant, beautiful, and alive. In fact, your desire for improvement can serve as an impetus for tremendous growth and development.

NBO creeps in, however, when your desires for improvement are motivated by a gnawing sense of inadequacy, a subtle belief that you are not quite wonderful the way you are. When your desires come from this place of inadequacy, your attempts to fulfill them are often thwarted or require tremendous effort. When you learn to fully befriend, accept, and love yourself, on the other hand, improvement can happen with patience, ease, and grace. When improvement comes from a place of acceptance and perfection, your potential for growth is unlimited. We'll talk more about this later.

> At your essence, you are beauty.

Isn't NBO Normal?

Negative Body Obsession has become such a mainstay of modern culture that you may think it's the only way to live. Many hardworking, bright people would agree with you—I have met some of them, in fact. As part of my own journey away from NBO, I had the pleasure of working with two different psychologists, both of whom I respect tremendously, at two separate times in my life. When discussing my concerns and angst about my body, they both told me that all women (and a growing number of men) in modern society struggle to some extent with dissatisfaction with their bodies. I was not surprised to hear that; I'd heard friends, family, and coworkers complain about their bodies, too.

> The reality is that *you* are enough; you are *more* than enough, right now, in this moment, regardless of *anything* and *everything* else.

What did bother me was that their statements implied that NBO was just the nature of life in modern society. It was just something I'd have to learn to live with. I could choose to continue my unhealthy obsessive angst or settle for a milder and more acceptable general form of dissatisfaction. Either way, love of my body and complete freedom from physical dissatisfaction was not mentioned as an option.

Although their insight and expertise helped me tremendously, there was always a small voice inside me that yearned for something more. Part of me knew that even if this discontent was "normal," it was not *natural*. There is nothing natural about:

- A gnawing discontent with your physical appearance
- Wanting to be somehow different so that you can feel beautiful, desirable, and successful
- Feeling dissatisfied every time you look in the mirror
- Believing that life would be better if you just weighed a little less or looked a little younger

On the contrary, what *is* natural is:

- The unshakable knowledge in your inherent beauty, goodness, and strength
- Experiencing yourself as inherently perfect
- Experiencing the peace and bliss of your own being
- Knowing that you are absolutely lovable in this very moment

So yes, Negative Body Obsession is "normal" and very common. But it is anything but natural.

The Costs of Living with Negative Body Obsession

Living with NBO exacts a tremendous toll on many aspects of your life. The costs can include compromised health, difficulty maintaining relationships, and the inability to make the progress you desire in life. NBO, no matter how subtle or how acute the condition, prevents you from living your life to the fullest. It encourages you to settle for mediocrity, instead of living the brilliance and glory that is your birthright.

Physical Tolls

If your Negative Body Obsession focuses on your weight, it can cause a difficult and frustrating relationship with food that can wreak havoc on your physical health and well-being.

NBO and Weight Loss

Consider this example. Say you decide to go on a diet. A number of scenarios might unfold:

1. **You lose weight.** But the diet is overly restrictive and you feel deprived, so you struggle the entire time. You eventually come off the diet and gain back the weight. (Statistics show that this happens to the vast majority of dieters.) You may try another diet, and another diet, and yet another diet, but never achieve the lasting results you want. You aren't happy with your body, and you feel resigned to either live with it or continue on the dieting merry-go-round. Your relationship with your weight is one of dissatisfaction, discontent, and dismay.

2. **You lose a healthy amount of weight but then spiral out of control.** At first, you feel great: you feel in control of your eating and in control of your life. You get a lot of satisfaction from the control and accomplishment. But then you lose weight beyond healthy levels and the once-innocent diet spirals into disordered eating. You may struggle with excessive food restriction, bingeing, and purging. If you do achieve and maintain a healthy body weight, you fail to achieve any lasting peace regarding food and your body, often feeling anxious and uneasy, afraid that you might lose control.

3. **You never seem to be able to restrict your food intake appropriately.** You discover bulimia, learning to purge after consuming food. You may be underweight, a normal weight, or overweight. Whatever the case, you don't feel like you can control what you eat. You overindulge (or simply believe that you overindulge even though you don't) and then purge in an attempt to right the wrong of overeating or eating at all.

4. **You turn to food as a source of comfort.** Maybe you struggle with depression and anxiety; maybe you experienced some form of childhood abuse. Maybe you have high stress levels or low energy levels. Whatever the case, you find that food offers adequate comfort, and you develop a habit of emotional and compulsive eating. You may have lost weight on many diets and then regained the weight, repeating this cycle many times throughout your life. You've never been able to establish a healthy, peaceful, easy rela-

tionship with food and your body. You often feel ashamed, embarrassed, and frustrated with your lack of success.

5. **You are chronically exhausted and overwhelmed.** Your life is depleting and exhausting. You can't handle one more thing such as losing weight or starting an exercise program. You stay overweight and out of shape. You dislike your body, often feel inadequate or ashamed, but just don't have the energy to get a diet program off the ground.

At least one of those scenarios sounds familiar, right? Many people go through a number, if not most, of these scenarios as they struggle with their body weight and physical appearance. Here is the sad truth: Negative Body Obsession will keep you trapped indefinitely in this cycle. No matter whether your weight is up or down or somewhere in between, you won't find peace or satisfaction. You'll have a gnawing sense of fear that you either cannot lose enough weight or are destined to gain it back. No matter where you are on the scale, you are not happy. The very best is a fleeting moment of satisfaction, soon to be eclipsed by this relentless fear.

You are beautiful, perfect, worthwhile, and lovable right now, in this moment.

NBO and Physical Appearance

Your Negative Body Obsession need not be about your weight, of course. Perhaps for you, NBO is focused on your dissatisfaction with a particular body part. For example, you dislike your wrinkles or your hair. Your nose is too big for your liking. Your breasts are too small; your feet are too flat. You have cellulite on the back of your thighs. Your list of perceived imperfections might be short or long and it may change over time.

To deal with the NBO, you might cover up the offending body part. You might hide it; try to ignore it. Whatever the case, NBO prevents you from feeling beautiful, brilliant, and radiant. You are ashamed of this part of your body, and in turn you project anger and even hatred toward it.

Emotional Pain

The costs of living with Negative Body Obsession are not only physical; they are also emotional and even spiritual. To better comprehend NBO's influence, it is helpful to understand the genesis of our emotions.

According to Carol Ritberger, PhD, a well-known author and medical intuitive, there are actually only two emotions: fear and love. Within these two emotions is the source of the seemingly endless array of emotions we experience. For example, fear is the root emotion of all negative responses, including phobias, panic disorders, post-traumatic stress disorder, obsessive-compulsive disorder, and, of course, NBO. Fear causes you to erect mental walls in an attempt to create a sense of security and protection. Instead of providing security, however, the walls rob you of joy and love and create a sense of separation and isolation that leads to emotional pain and suffering.

How NBO Is Based in Fear

Living with NBO is living with this chronic fear. The fear is rooted in the feeling that you are not quite good enough. You may be surrounded by friends, yet your feelings of inadequacy prevent you from experiencing truly intimate connections. If you feel unattractive and unworthy, or embarrassed and ashamed, that part of you is isolated from others. This fear-based isolation compounds feelings of loneliness, which can force you to turn to or avoid food as a means of coping.

Live a life of *love* instead of a life of *fear.*

Connecting the Physical and the Emotional

In order to combat the fear, your mind convinces you that the problem is with your body. If you just weighed less, looked better, and didn't have that darn cellulite, everything would be okay—or at least it would be better. This erroneous belief causes you to fixate on your body, thinking that's where you will find peace, joy, and comfort.

Unfortunately, this negative relationship you have with your body forces you to live with a closed heart since you are afraid to let others in to see your alleged "flaws." Living with a closed heart limits your relationships, limits your potential, and stunts your emotional growth. And that is no way to live.

Indeed, life with an *open* heart is the only life worth living. It is the only way you can experience your glory, your beauty, and your strength.

Spiritual Pain

Beyond the physical and emotional costs of NBO lies the damage done on the spiritual front. Now let me clarify—you can't actually damage your spirit because it is a timeless, boundless, part of yourself. But tremendous suffering occurs when you are unaware of your spiritual truth. Living with NBO prevents you from experiencing who you truly are. We should all have the joy of fulfilling our timeless, boundless, limitless potential. NBO deprives you of this fundamental experience. NBO makes you believe that you *are* your body and that your well-being is dependent on your body looking a certain way. You are set up to fail by grounding your happiness in the wrong place.

The Solution Is Only a Thought Away

Yes, Negative Body Obsession is a pervasive problem that affects every aspect of your being. Fortunately, however, you can eradicate NBO from your life. I know that this may sound impossible, but it's not. The way out of this suffering is to shift your awareness from a small, finite, ego-based reality to one of unlimited, eternal, and abundant love. You will discover that you do not need to prop yourself up by looking a certain way or accomplishing a certain thing. Instead, you will realize that you are already whole, beautiful, and perfect, just as you are right now.

NBO, and the suffering it has caused in your life, is not the only way to live. You are not limited to the unhealthy body-mind connection that is the source of your struggle, angst, and pain. You are not an isolated, broken, lonely person, although that might very well be your experience at the moment.

> Self-acceptance is not an invitation for complacency. It is the doorway to fulfilling your *grandest dreams* and *greatest desires*.

In reality, you are eternal, omnipotent, and omnipresent. You are the brilliance of the entire universe manifesting as a single human being. That sounds pretty amazing, doesn't it? It might sound almost silly to hear that at this point in your struggle—you likely can't imagine yourself with such grandeur—but over the course of this book, you'll see that it's true. You'll see that your greatness, your joy, and your peace, are far more real than the suffering that may characterize your life with NBO.

Get Acclimated with Your Spiritual Side

One fundamental premise of this book is that healing from Negative Body Obsession requires shifting your awareness from small, finite, ego-based reality to limitless, pure, unbounded potential. There will be many exercises and activities throughout this book designed to help you do just that. You can begin immediately, however, to shift your awareness.

Take the time right now to repeat these phrases out loud and begin the process of reclaiming your true identity. No need to worry if you have a difficult time understanding these statements; just begin to repeat them to yourself, out loud and silently. As you progress through subsequent chapters you will gain a deeper understanding of your true nature and become intimately familiar with these concepts.

- At my essence, I am beauty.
- My true nature is an infinite field of pure potential and limitless possibility.
- My beauty is eternal.
- I am the creator of my life and my experiences.
- I am inherently lovable, beautiful, and worthwhile regardless of my body size, shape, or color.
- I have the power within me to create a life that I love.
- I am love.

Points to Remember

- We are in the midst of an epidemic—an epidemic of Negative Body Obsession.
- Sufferers of NBO go through life never feeling beautiful enough, strong enough, sexy enough, or perfect enough to live their lives fully.
- The reality is that you are enough; you are more than enough, right now, in this moment, regardless of anything and everything else.
- At your essence, you are beauty.
- Self-acceptance is not an invitation for complacency. It is the doorway to fulfilling your grandest dreams and greatest desires.
- If your diet stems from a belief that you are not quite good enough the way you are, it is doomed to fail.
- There is nothing wrong with the desire to change and improve, nor is there anything wrong with the desire to stay the same.
- When desires are motivated by inadequacy, they are much more difficult to fulfill.
- When you befriend, accept, and love yourself unconditionally, you remove barriers to evolution and the fulfillment of your desires.
- Shifting your identity from ego-based individuality to universal Source is the path for alleviating suffering.

CHAPTER TWO

How Did This Happen? How We Learned to Hate Our Bodies

Now that you know what Negative Body Obsession is, it is helpful to understand where it came from. Unearthing the causes of NBO will help you lay the groundwork to overcome it.

So, what causes NBO? Is it the media, with its obsession and idealization of thin? Is your brain wired wrong? Is it the fault of computers and fast-food chains that make you eat more and move less? Is it the fault of your parents or teachers? Is it loneliness? Who or what can we blame for this sorry situation?

Contributing Factors That *Aren't* the Main Cause

Unfortunately, there's no easy answer. Yes, all those factors can and do contribute to Negative Body Obsession. None of them, however, is the root cause. They are instead symptoms of an underlying problem. Let's look at each:

- **Media:** Yes, most media promotes a limited idealization of beauty. But society created and continues to endorse the media by watching shows that highlight the false ideals and buying weekly entertainment magazines that feature photo after photo of too-thin stars. So who exactly can we fault for the media's focus? Those who create the media? Those who watch, read, or listen to the media? Those who believe the media?

> Our experience and beliefs *about the world* reflect our experience and beliefs *about ourselves*.

- **Your brain:** What if your brain is just wired in a way that makes you hate your body? Believe it or not, there is some validity to that idea. Experts have conducted brain-imaging scans, which reveal amazing data on how our brains work and why some people suffer from anorexia, bulimia, or compulsive eating, while others live without such problems. (We'll talk about this more on page 20.) Even so, you can change how your brain works; you can quite literally heal injured, overworked, and underworked parts of your brain.

- **Fast food/computers:** Yes, fast-food chains and sedentary lifestyles have not helped Americans achieve health and fitness. However, you probably know strong, vital, and healthy people who spend hours in front of a computer or flying in airplanes. They manage to balance these lifestyle challenges.

- **Your parents:** This is an easy one, right? It must be your parents' fault. Well, yes, your parents—consciously or unconsciously—might have given you many negative thoughts, beliefs, and behaviors that have created tremendous suffering. But they were only passing on the thoughts, beliefs, and behaviors that were true for them.

The bottom line is that each of these circumstances is simply a manifestation of a fundamental flaw in the way we think of, perceive, and live reality.

So What Is the Real Cause?

The root cause of NBO is not realizing that each and every one of us is intrinsically beautiful and inherently valuable exactly as we are, right now. That's it. Every other cause stems from this fundamental error.

If we all lived from this place of truth and reality, we would create a world that reflected this. We would create media that reflected this. We would create a society that encouraged and promoted this realization. Unfortunately, most people live from a place of delusion and illusion, believing that they need to change something or hold on to something in order to be beautiful, desirable, adequate, and worthwhile, and this is what we see reflected in our culture.

Your reality is a projection of your consciousness, including your beliefs, your attitudes, and your behaviors. Since most people accept a standard of beauty that is based on a limited ideal, you have probably created a reality in which that ideal must be met in order for you to achieve success and happiness. Let's take a closer look at what creates your idea of beauty.

The History of Beauty

We know the ideal that twenty-first-century America has set forth. However, it's important to realize that beauty, or attractiveness, is a socially constructed phenomenon that changes constantly. As societies evolve and change, so does their concept of the "ideal" body. What is considered beautiful is both created and informed by changing thoughts and opinions.

Before the beginning of the twentieth century, attractive female bodies had ample curves and were not particularly toned according to modern standards. Think back to art you've seen in museums. What was once considered beautiful and desirable would now be considered overweight. You have no doubt seen women in Western paintings from 1400 to 1900 with rolls of fat and cellulite (think of works by Rubens, Botticelli, and Renoir). Their breasts fall naturally; their pelvises are large; their stomachs are soft. In the modern-day ideal, however, we see ribs, muscles, and bony protrusions.

There are many reasons for these changing images of beauty. Historically, being fat was considered a status symbol. Only the affluent could afford luxurious meals, so a heavy body was indicative of financial success. In modern-day developed nations, however, food is abundant, and the heavy ideal has been replaced with the thin ideal. A study by Judith L. Anderson at Simon Fraser University in 1992 showed that people who don't worry about getting enough food would rather have a slim figure. Another study, by Nigel Barber at the Birmingham-Southern College in 1998, claims that a woman's livelihood plays a role in how her society prefers her body size. In cultures where women primarily have domestic roles, people appear to prefer heavier figures. In cultures where women are involved politically and economically, people appear to prefer slender figures.

Muscular bodies used to betray the fact that a person had to perform manual labor, putting him or her in a lower societal class. Rich people could avoid that type of work and were therefore often untoned. Nowadays, however, machines do much of the work that used to be manual. Only those with the spare time (and in some cases, money) are fit, and a more muscular look has become desirable.

The point of this discussion is to realize that what's considered "beautiful" at any given moment is fleeting and somewhat arbitrary. For various reasons, society simply decides that a certain look is beautiful. The question is: Do you want to be subject to the ever-changing whims of cultural preference? Do you want to accept a vision of beauty that deems some people are attractive, while others are not? Or do you want to know that you are beautiful no matter what time period or country you live in?

The Media's Influence

As we discussed, the media certainly has exacerbated the NBO epidemic. We are bombarded with images of predominantly thin women and muscular men. Fashion designers claim that clothing is showcased better on thin models, so most models are tall and rail thin, and most clothes are designed for people with that body shape. (Of course, those clothes don't fit the majority of the population.)

You probably look at those idealized and airbrushed models and think that you should look like that. You've probably also heard the reality: the average American woman wears a size 14, which is a far cry from the size 2 or 4 most models wear. Advertising leads you to believe that if you look a certain way—which is of course different from how you currently appear—you too would have the sexy partner, the great house, the fabulous clothes, and the exciting lifestyle. In essence, you would finally be happy and successful.

In order to view ourselves and others in a *positive* way, we must identify and detach from the *negative* and *delusional* thought patterns that have been passed down through *society*.

The truth is that you can decide what stories you allow into your mind. You can choose what you believe to be true. It is only when you uncover and uproot the ultimate illusion—that you need to change in order to be beautiful, lovable, and worthwhile—that you can begin to change yourself, the media, and ultimately the world around you.

When you confirm that beauty comes in many different shapes, sizes, ages, and ethnicities, you will experience this to be true. If enough people live like this, it will be reflected in the media, in advertising, and in every other sector of society.

Your Brain's Reactions

Since we can influence what we choose to view and believe, what's the connection between NBO and your brain? Are you just wired incorrectly?

The groundbreaking work of Daniel Amen, MD, on brain imaging has helped to shed some light on the subject. His brain scans show which areas are active at any given moment. He has a database of 50,000 scans, so he can compare a particular scan with many others to identify trends. He found that the brain images of many people with eating disorders, including compulsive eating, show certain parts of the brain are overactive. Their brains could be causing them to react to food in a certain way.

Dr. Amen is also quick to point out, however, that you are not stuck with the brain patterns you were born with, nor with the brain patterns that you have developed throughout your life. You can actually *change your brain*. As you will learn in Step 2, Identifying and Detaching from Negative Thoughts, you can use the power of your thoughts to rewire your brain. If you live with the mindset that you need to change in order to be beautiful, lovable, or worthwhile, you are programming your brain for anxiety, insecurity, and angst. What if you can't change? What if you don't change? What if you are never quite good enough? This destructive thinking could create anxiety and disordered eating in even the most balanced of people.

On the other hand, by taking an active role in directing your thoughts, you can change the way that your neurons fire. Over time, you can change and improve the structure of your brain. Imagine if you knew deep down that you were already perfect, that there was no need to do, have, or become anything other than what you already are. There would be no room in your life for anxiety, angst, or misery. This positive thought, this belief, this knowledge of reality would help you create a healthy brain.

Overcoming Influence—Confronting Mass Media

Now, you might be thinking that I am underestimating the power of the media. You might protest, "How can I stop being influenced by the media that is everywhere? I walk into a grocery store and see magazine after magazine with pictures of airbrushed models, along with articles about which star has gained or lost weight. I turn on my TV and see advertisement after advertisement offering the latest diet so that I can fit into my favorite pair of jeans. I listen to my friends talk about who has lost weight and how great she looks. How in the world can I ignore these influences?"

Here is an exercise to help you talk back to these media influences. When you master the art of talking back, you can reclaim your control and become an influencer of the media, instead of being a victim influenced by the media.

Step 1: Become Aware of Your Reaction

Whenever you find yourself looking at media, immediately become aware of your reaction. Let's say, for example, you are standing in the grocery store looking at the cover of a magazine. The magazine is showing the latest pop star who has either gained weight or lost weight. If she has gained weight, it is considered a crisis and she is considered less beautiful. If she has lost weight, she is heralded as triumphant and stunning. Notice how you react to this. Is your first impulse to agree with the magazine, thinking, "Wow, yes, she looks much better thinner," or "I wonder how she let herself get like that?" or "I wish I could have her thin body!" or "I wonder how her boyfriend feels about her body?" The first step is to simply become aware of your reaction to the media influence, in this case the magazine cover.

Step 2: Question Your Reaction

The next step is to question your reaction. Why do you believe that thinner is inherently more attractive? Where did that belief come from? Why accept that the media knows anything about what is attractive? Or about what makes someone successful, lovable, beautiful, or worthwhile? Is there any reason to believe the media knows what it is talking about? What if you had a different reaction? Could you just as easily believe that the media is offering *a* vision of beauty, not *the* vision of beauty? And could you choose to embody a different vision in your own life? Don't take anything at face value—notice how you are being influenced, and then question your habitual reaction.

Step 3: Think of Evidence to the Contrary

The third step in breaking free from media influence is to think of evidence to the contrary. For example, we have already discussed how beauty has changed throughout the ages, so there is evidence that there is nothing inherently more beautiful about being thin. Can you think of women who don't fit into the western beauty ideal yet are nonetheless stunning? Summon to mind people whom you consider beautiful for reasons that have nothing to do with the size or shape of their bodies.

Can you think of women who are financially successful who don't have svelte bodies? Or how about women in a loving, intimate relationship? I bet you can. You see, there is no necessary correlation between the size of your body and achieving the success and love you desire. This is a belief system that you might have adopted, but there is no inherent truth to it, and you can make the choice right now to identify the fallacy for what it is.

Step 4: Talk Back!

That's right—it is time to talk back to the media and the beliefs that have been fed to you without your knowledge. You have become aware of your reaction, you have questioned your reaction, and you have found evidence to debunk your erroneous assumptions. Now you can look at the media and say "Wait a second—I see you for what you are! You are projecting a limited vision of beauty. You are promoting a vision that does not encompass the depth and breadth of true beauty. I have assumed that what you promoted was true, and now I see that it is simply one view, and it is a view that does not strengthen, edify, or empower the many faces of beauty that are around me all the time. I don't need to accept your vision of beauty; I don't need to follow your erroneous path for success. I am choosing, right now, in this moment, to define beauty on my terms. I am going to set the standards for what is attractive, and it is going to be a vision that encompasses the true beauty of humanity."

In this way, you can talk back to the media. By talking back, by questioning what you are being told and setting a new standard, you become a creator and an influencer, instead of being controlled by the images and stories that come into your life every day.

So yes, your brain *can* influence your behavior and be a cause of an uncomfortable relationship with food and your body. However, if you shift your reality from one of feeling inadequate to one where you know you are already beautiful and inherently worthwhile, you will begin to heal your brain.

The Impact of Fast Food

Perhaps Negative Body Obsession is simply the result of living in a nation where a large percent of the population is obese. The news is replete with stories about the obesity epidemic: children are overweight; diabetes diagnoses are at an all-time high. The average American's lifestyle is sedentary, and people spend more time than ever sitting in front of a computer or TV screen.

There are very serious health consequences from being overweight, just as there are very serious health complications from being underweight.

But can we really blame NBO on the availability of unhealthy fast food and a sedentary lifestyle? After all, plenty of people in America are healthy and fit, and able to maintain a healthy body weight without living in fear and obsession. Between the McDonald's on almost every corner and ads for fast food on practically every TV show, there is no doubt that unhealthy food is a deterrent to our health and fitness goals.

But you can take control of your choices and your actions to negate this force. When you start from the premise that you are inherently beautiful, lovable, and worthwhile, you can make diet and lifestyle choices that affirm this. Diet and lifestyle choices that you make from a place of love and acceptance have a far greater chance of success than ones premised on shame and inadequacy. Self-acceptance and self-love provide you with the courage, the energy, and the enthusiasm to make choices that move you further in the direction of health and well-being.

It's Not (Entirely) Your Parent's Fault . . .

Without question, your childhood and upbringing have a significant impact on your self-view today. Did your parents give you unconditional love? Did they encourage you? Did they compliment you?

As little children, we are as dependent on our parents' love as we are on food and water for our survival. We desperately need them to affirm our perfection, to see and acknowledge our beauty and our brilliance. Think of children at the playground, calling "Watch me! Watch me!" or proudly showing off a finger-painting project. When parents give the affection, children learn to see themselves in the same positive light. They grow up knowing that they are inherently perfect, radiant, and beautiful. They grow up knowing that they are capable of anything.

Unfortunately, few people struggling with NBO received this unconditional love and acknowledgment as children. Most of us learned to operate with *conditional* love and acceptance. We learned that we needed to look a certain way, behave in a certain way, and be a certain way in order to get the love and affection we desired. We learned how to contort ourselves, diminish ourselves, and change ourselves so that we could receive the approval and affection from our parents that we wanted and needed so badly. We learned early on that receiving love meant changing something about ourselves. We then learned to love ourselves in this same conditional way. We began to accept ourselves if and only if we looked or acted a certain way. In so doing, we lost touch with the unconditional love that is always there, always waiting, and always available.

Even though your parents' actions may have contributed to your current situation, they are, however, not to blame. They could not truly affirm your beauty and perfection because they probably did not experience themselves that way. Most likely, they had not been raised to see their inherent perfection either. As a result, they simply raised you in a way that reflected their own state of awareness and their experience of reality.

It is only possible to accept others unconditionally when you accept yourself unconditionally. It is only possible to experience others as beautiful, whole, and perfect, when you experience yourself as beautiful, whole, and perfect. Your parents were likely unable to do that. Fortunately, when you learn how to love yourself unconditionally, you will be able to extend this same love and acceptance to everyone around you. As you do this, you will reinforce your own intrinsic beauty and perfection as well.

The Choice Is Yours

Although there are a variety of contributing factors, NBO has ultimately been caused and perpetuated by an erroneous reality that places your sense of self-worth in how you look, what you have, and what other people think about you.

Here's the good news: once you know the cause, you can find the solution. The solution comes from deciding to change your thought patterns and create a different reality. You will realize that you are, always were, and always will be inherently beautiful, lovable, and worthwhile. When you are able to experience this sensation, you can make whatever changes you want to make. As you come to truly know yourself, your reaction to the media will change; your brain will be healed; you can break free from any limiting beliefs, thoughts, and behaviors that are keeping you trapped. Once the fundamental error is identified and debunked, you can create a life of peace, joy, and abundance.

> We can only view and treat others as *inherently lovable*, *beautiful*, and *valuable* if we view and treat ourselves that way.

Points to Remember

- There are many causes or reasons for Negative Body Obsession, but all of them stem from one fundamental error.
- This error is not realizing that each and every one of us is intrinsically beautiful and inherently valuable exactly as we are, right now.
- Our experience and beliefs about the world reflect our experience and beliefs about ourselves.
- We can only view and treat others as inherently lovable, beautiful, and valuable if we view and treat ourselves this way.
- In order to view ourselves and others in this way, we must identify and detach from the negative and delusional thought patterns that have been passed down through society.

CHAPTER THREE

A Vision of the Possible: Life Without NBO

Can you imagine a time when you won't hate your body? When you won't compare yourself to other people you see, or wish your body was different in some way? If you've suffered from Negative Body Obsession for a long time, it's probably difficult to do. Yet there is no need to despair. True genius comes from envisioning what is possible but has not yet been experienced or even explored. "Geniuses" have a dream of what they want to create and focus on it, letting go of any thoughts, beliefs, and behaviors to the contrary. Luckily, you are a true genius!

Adopting that mindset is how you can break free from NBO, and create change in any area of your life. You won't create change in your life by contemplating what you *don't* want. Airplanes were not developed by thinking about how things stayed on the ground. This concept sounds simple, but really think about it. You probably spend most of your time thinking about what you *don't* have and what you *aren't*. In order to live without NBO, you need to imagine what you could have.

Now that you understand the nature and history of NBO, contemplate its opposite. The more you focus on NBO itself, the more you will attract it into your life. On the other hand, the more you contemplate a life of peace with your body, the more you focus on loving and accepting your body and enjoying it as an ally on your journey through life, the more you will create those feelings in your life.

In order to change your life, you must first change your mind. Since it is difficult to imagine something that you have not yet experienced, this chapter shows you a blueprint of what life looks like without NBO. We'll follow the fictional Cassandra through a typical day breaking free from NBO. Some of her thoughts and reactions may sound familiar to you. Notice, however, how she employs a healthy, loving mindset to combat any negative feelings that arise.

A Day on the Path to Freedom

Cassandra wakes up in the morning and smiles. She feels energetic and alive, excited to explore the adventure that this day will bring. She quietly says thank you to the universe for her restful night's sleep, for her very comfortable bed and soft pillows, and for the cool dream she had about successfully completing a mountain-climbing expedition.

She gets up, goes to the bathroom to brush her teeth, and then sits down in her most comfortable chair for her daily meditation. Her meditation is routine—it includes thoughts about what she is going to do that day, what she ate for dinner last night, what exercise routine she will choose today, and whether or not she remembered to call her brother on his birthday. She feels relaxed and energized after her meditation and makes her way to the kitchen for breakfast.

She grabs her usual breakfast: a slice of toast with nut butter, some fresh berries, and a glass of milk. Her mind instantaneously calculates the calories in her meal, trying to decipher whether this is an appropriate amount of food. She feels an inkling of anxiety begin to creep in, as she starts to worry about whether she will lose weight or gain weight, and what she should eat later in the day, based on her morning meal.

She smiles and thinks, "Oh isn't that cute, my habituated thought pattern, repeating the same old thing. Good thing I don't have to listen to that. I will pick a better thought that will make me feel better right now."

She chooses this one: "I am so glad I have food readily available to me in the morning. Studies have shown that eating breakfast boosts metabolism throughout the whole day. I am grateful that I have the opportunity to eat this healthy breakfast that is going to provide me with energy and sustenance throughout the entire day.

"Furthermore, I know that I am beautiful. I know that I am capable of making healthy choices regarding food and my body. I know that I can create the fitness, health, and beauty that I desire. It might take a little bit of time for my body to find its healthy balance because I have been depriving it for a long while, but that's okay. I have all the time in the world, and I know that I am beautiful, lovable, and worthwhile regardless of my body size."

The short, silent, mental dialogue lasts only a matter of seconds, but Cassandra feels much better. As the bread heats up in the toaster, she is now looking forward to her favorite breakfast, a truly delicious and satisfying meal.

After breakfast, she gets ready to shower before work. As she takes her clothes off, she notices herself avoiding looking in the mirror. She senses a concern that she might have gained weight, since she is no longer rigidly "dieting." She habitually squeezes in her stomach and notices herself concerned that the inside of her thighs are touching. When she becomes aware of this, she once again smiles.

"How boring my mind can be," she muses, "constantly worried about the same old thing!" She stops what she is doing and turns to face her naked body in the mirror. A thought deluge comes: "Oh my gosh, you really need to eat less. Your thighs are completely out of proportion with the rest of your body. You are gaining weight—there is no way you will fit into your favorite jeans!" Cassandra winces as she listens to the tirade. She takes a deep breath, looks at her eyes in the mirror, and has a quick dialogue with herself.

"I can see, habituated mind, that you are concerned about how I look. I understand that you are deeply afraid that I am no longer rigidly controlling my food intake. You know, I really appreciate you looking out for me and being concerned for my welfare. The fact is I am more than capable of taking care of myself. I no longer need your assistance. I am setting an intention to have a healthy, fit body and a peaceful relationship with food. I really don't need your help anymore. Thanks, though."

Cassandra then speaks to herself, using the voice of wisdom, "You know, I am truly beautiful. My body was made exactly as it was meant to be. If I can't see my beauty right now, the problem is not with my body; it is with my eyes. I intend to discover and experience my beauty, every day, all the time." Cassandra then gently caresses her stomach and thighs with loving affection and jumps in the shower.

She feels exquisitely proud of herself for relying on her wisdom and trusting in her own greatness. This whole process took no longer than a few moments—she is becoming quite adept at identifying her thoughts and immediately telling a different story. While showering, she congratulates herself on how far she has come.

While driving to work, Cassandra listens to some of her favorite music, which lifts her mood and gets her ready for the day. She is stuck in traffic for longer than usual, so she puts in an inspirational CD of daily affirmations, offering gratitude for the extra time for learning and growth.

Once at work, she is inundated with her usual barrage of tasks. She has fifty e-mails to read, ten voice mails to return, and learns that her dry cleaning has been lost and her rent check mysteriously disappeared in the mail.

It is lunchtime before she is able to take a breath. She devours the wholesome lunch that she brought with her—steamed veggies, brown rice, and fish—in a matter of minutes. She unconsciously reaches for a doughnut that someone had brought for a morning meeting and proceeds to inhale the whole thing without thinking twice.

She is suddenly shaken as if from a dream and realizes what she had done. She looks at the few remaining crumbs and feels her breathing stop from fear. "Oh no! What have I done?" she silently thinks to herself. She feels an impulse to run to the bathroom and purge. Part of her wants to leap up from her chair to rush straight to the toilet. Another part of her cements her butt to the chair. Her fear is palpable; her desire to purge is intense.

Yet she catches herself, her wisdom stepping in and gently coaxing her down from the precipice of her fear. She says to herself, "It's okay. Your body will digest this doughnut and extract all the nutrients it can. Tomorrow you will gently limit your sugar intake. There is absolutely nothing to worry about. Everyone has days like these. Breathe, breathe. It is going to be perfectly okay. I love you. You are doing an incredible job. Breathe, breathe."

Cassandra takes a few deep breaths. She checks in with her stomach. Although she is full, she is not stuffed. "It is all going to be all right," she reassures herself as she heads back to work.

After work, Cassandra drives straight to the gym. She is looking forward to her workout as a much-needed stress release from an exhausting day. She does her meditation while seated in the car, before heading in for her Spin class. Her exercise generates large amounts of endorphins and she feels great by the end of her workout. She overhears two women lamenting about how much they ate at a party the night before. She is tempted to berate herself for the doughnut earlier that day but makes a conscious choice to offer herself love and acceptance instead.

After the gym, she heads home and thinks about what she will have for dinner. She is not very hungry, so chooses to eat a light bowl of soup. She catches up on e-mail after dinner, takes a quick shower, and gets ready for bed.

Once in bed, she mentally reviews her day. She runs through everything that has happened, reminding herself that she is great and powerful and can respond appropriately to any challenges. After a quick mental review, she cannot help but smile.

She was exposed to the same pressures she had always faced. She saw the same people, she heard the same comments. She listened to the people around her judging other people's bodies. Sometimes she ate super-healthily, and other times not so much. And it didn't matter so much either way. She realized that no one had the power to make her feel a certain way. She was able to maintain her well-being, no matter what anyone said. She knew that when she sometimes ate too much, she would be able to bring it into balance over the next few days. She sensed within her a growing conviction that no matter what life sends her way, she can always find a way to succeed. She knows that at her essence she is beautiful, lovable, and worthwhile.

Taking Stock of Cassandra's Life

She seems pretty stable, healthy, and happy, doesn't she? Every day that Cassandra practices in this way, she has fewer thoughts about her inadequacy. Her habitual negative dialogue begins to fall away. Her worrying about food intake, her calorie counting, and her relentless dialogue about proper food gradually begin to disappear. Meanwhile, her positive inner dialogue becomes second nature. Her affirmations and active self-love become programmed into her mind so that they run on their own accord, just as her negative thoughts had done.

Her experience of herself as radiant, beautiful, and glorious gradually becomes a habit. When she looks in the mirror, there is no voice that suggests she should be thinner. When she sees her reflection, no part of her cringes with fear. She threw away her bathroom scale because she realized it served no purpose whatsoever. Judgment about how she should look, how she is aging, or what clothing size she is wearing slowly faded away.

Over time, her first and only response becomes one of love, acceptance, and appreciation. When she looks in the mirror, she sees her brilliance. When she looks at her friends, she sees their divinity. Everywhere she looks, she sees only beauty; she sees only love. When she sees someone new, her first thought is of his or her beauty. With time, everywhere she turns, she feels love. Most importantly, she feels that love toward herself, every day, all the time.

Breaking Free

Whether you are a middle-aged man or woman carrying a little more weight than you would like, an emotional eater, someone struggling with obesity, someone suffering from anorexia or bulimia, or a teenager dreaming of being the latest pop star, you can break free from Negative Body Obsession. You can live a positive, healthy life like Cassandra.

The following chapters explain a five-step process to end your relationship with NBO and claim the life of your dreams. The strategies will launch you on the path to self-love and self-acceptance, helping to make Cassandra's reality your reality. Apply each step diligently, practice each of the exercises, apply yourself with zeal and enthusiasm, stay unwavering in the face of setbacks, and you will be able to break free and realize your greatest potential and lasting beauty. As the famous saying goes, "Change the way you look at things, and the things you look at will change."

Points to Remember

- Successful change begins with a vision. Start to imagine what your ideal life would look like living without NBO.
- Breaking free is often a process. There is no need to despair if you find yourself revisiting negative patterns. Learning how to combat habitual tendencies on a regular basis is the key to long-term success.
- Develop a practice of becoming aware and changing your thoughts in each moment. As the old saying goes, "Rome was not built in a day." You are creating new habits and they will become ingrained as you practice them on a consistent and regular basis.
- There is one true force in the world and it is love. Focus on treating yourself with love in any and every situation.
- Consistently look at what a life free of NBO looks like for you. As you regularly review the list you made, you will begin to create it in your life.

What Does Your Life of Freedom Look Like?

Take the time right now to imagine what your life of freedom will look like. What will your ideal day look like when you successfully break free from NBO? Remember, success is not limited to the final result. It is being engaged in the process in a loving, healthy, positive way. When you are fully engaged in the process, the final result will eventually and effortlessly come. Here are some suggestions to get you started.

When I successfully break free, I will:

- Look in the mirror with love, appreciation, affection, and gratitude.
- Develop an overall healthy way of eating and exercising that has adequate room for indulgences, fun, and pleasure.
- Be gentle, loving, and kind with myself even if I confront apparent setbacks.
- Develop a habit of consciously and continuously detaching from negative thoughts, while creating more positive thoughts to put in their place.
- Become a beacon of hope, light, and beauty that is independent of the good or bad opinion of others.

- _____

- _____

- _____

- _____

- _____

- _____

CHAPTER FIVE

What Are Intentions?

As preparation for the five-step process, I want to introduce you to the idea of intention. If you're already familiar with it, great—let this chapter serve as a refresher course. If you're not, this chapter gives you the information you need to understand this concept.

Everything that you see in your life began with an intention, whether it was a conscious one or not. Intention has transformational power; it is the organizing principle behind all creativity. When you properly understand intention, you discover that you can create anything in your life, provided that you stay connected to the field of intention from which everything emanates.

Connecting with intention, ultimately, is effortless. When you connect with this field, you trust that your desires will be fulfilled. You simply align yourself with nature and hold on, trusting that you will be led to your destination.

As you can probably imagine, very few people live with this effortless ease. By now you might be feeling incredulous: Sarah Maria, what are you talking about?! I can manifest my desires *without* strain and struggle? This is an understandable question, since living with NBO has likely been a constant struggle thus far in your life. Let me explain . . . .

What Is Intention?

Intention is the force that animates and orchestrates everything in the universe without effort and without strain. It is a law or principle of the universe and it exists whether or not you decide to access its power.

Everything in the world is the result of intention.

In Dr. Wayne Dyer's book *The Power of Intention*, he explains that intention is not something you *do*. Rather, it is a force of the cosmos: it is what causes a seed to become an oak tree or a flower to blossom. It is what causes your hair to grow, your heart to beat, and your cells to regenerate. It is what animates your existence, gently and effortlessly developing you on every level, from a zygote to an embryo to a fetus, to a baby, child, adolescent, and adult. You don't actively think about any of those processes on a daily basis, yet they happen on their own. That's the ongoing influence of intention.

Here are some other key attributes of intention:

- Intention is all-inclusive. There is nowhere that it is not and nothing it does not include.
- Intention is always on time. It provides what the universe needs, when it needs it.

We usually refer to intention as being a "field"—as in "the field of intention." Think of it like the atmosphere. You might not see it, but it's always there, working in its own perfect rhythm.

What Is a Specific Intention?

A specific intention is how you connect with the field of intention. It is your way to tap into the organizing power that is inherent in the universe.

As already explained, everything in the world is evolving and developing, being influenced by this field of intention. When you set a specific, individual intention, it allows you to step into the flowing field of intention, which will gradually carry you to your desired destination.

You will use the power of your mind to create a specific intention to break free from NBO and claim the grand, glorious, beautiful life that you deserve. The intention will then just do its job, provided you complete the other exercises and practices in this book. Your intention will gradually move you in the direction of living a healthy, happy life, free from NBO and its accompanying stress, frustration, and angst.

> Through the *power* of intention, you can create *a life that you love.*

Scientific Studies in Intention

Those of you who aren't in close contact with your spiritual side may be thinking, "What a bunch of baloney! I can't make myself love my body by just thinking it will be so and letting the universe and its field of intention just 'take care of it'!" Let me appeal to your rational side with some scientific research to back up my claim.

Throughout history, most human beings have thought that reality is something outside of themselves that is independent of their thoughts and feelings. Most figured that what happens is somehow predetermined and immune from our influence. Well, it turns out that is not the case.

Quantum Physics (Yes, You Read That Right)

With the advent of quantum physics (which explores the nature and behavior of matter and energy on the atomic and subatomic level) in the early 1900s, a shift in scientific thinking occurred. (Yep, I am now talking about quantum physics. I *told* you this would be unlike any body-image book you've ever read! Bear with me; this is fascinating research!) Research has shown that (in the quantum realm, at least) an observer can actually influence what she is observing. Quantum physicists have discovered that at the quantum level, reality exists as a potential that will only manifest when it is observed.

According to Heisenberg's Uncertainty Principle (a key theorem in quantum physics—feel free to bring it up at your next cocktail party), a wave-particle (a particular unit) is both a wave and a particle at the same time. It remains in this state of possibility until an observer seeks to determine either its location or its momentum. Depending on what the observer is wanting to determine, it will collapse into either a wave or a particle. Until the moment of observation, it existed as potentially a wave or potentially a particle. At the moment of observation it collapsed into being one or the other. Quantum physics is confirming that reality, at least at the quantum level, exists as pure potential, a state of all possibilities, until the moment of observation. This might sound complex, I know. But really it is quite simple. Imagine that you are deciding whether to get Chinese food or Japanese food for dinner. Before the moment you make a decision, your future reality exists as pure possibility. You could go to a Chinese restaurant or a Japanese restaurant, or perhaps even an Italian restaurant, a Mediterranean restaurant, a French restaurant, or you could go to the grocery store, or forgo your meal altogether and do something completely different. The future restaurant exists as a possibility until the moment that you make a decision. Once you make a decision, the restaurant becomes Chinese or Japanese, depending on the choice you made.

Always affirm your inherent *goodness*, value, and *beauty*.

Research in the 1960s

Many scientists began to ask questions: If the act of observing determines outcomes at the quantum level, can it determine outcomes in everyday reality? If human beings can influence events in the quantum realm, can they also influence events in the physical world? As it turns out, yes!

Some of the first studies involving human intention sought to discover whether human beings could influence otherwise completely random events. In 1965, a man named Helmut Schmidt created a machine that had completely random output. For the sake of simplicity, think of the machine as a bubble machine, with the output being bubbles.

> Detach from the outcome, *trusting* that the *universe* will carry you where you want to go.

Bubble production was random, occurring without any particular order or rhythm. The goal was to determine whether human intention could have an ordering effect on the machine's behavior. Using the example above, could a participant influence bubble production through intention? If participants were shown to alter any element of the machine's output, he could conclude that they had influenced the probabilities of events, and thus that they had influenced the creation of reality by using their intention.

Amazingly, Schmidt discovered that these observers did, in fact, influence the machine! By merely intending, they could affect the machine output. To use the same metaphor, they could influence bubble creation so that it was no longer completely random. They could bring some kind of order to the bubble production to a degree that was beyond statistical chance.

More Recent Intention Research

Robert Jahn and Brenda Dunne continued Schmidt's experimentation at Princeton University in the 1980s. They wanted to discover if ordinary, everyday people with no psychic abilities whatsoever could influence the outcome of the random-output machine. (Many of Schmidt's intenders had documented psychic abilities and prowess.)

Jahn first improved upon Schmidt's machine, creating what came to be known as a Random Event Generator. Think again of the bubble machine, only this was a new, improved version. This machine was constructed to guarantee that any deviation from the normal 50-50 chance would be due only to human influence on the machine. The output was coded as either IS or OS (think big bubble or small bubble). They had each participant sit in front of the machine and conduct three experiments of equal length:

1. The person would attempt to get the machine to produce more IS than OS.
2. The person would intend for more OS than IS.
3. The person would not attempt to influence the machine in any way.

After 5,000 studies, Jahn and Dunne tabulated their results. They used red dots for any time the operator had attempted to influence the machine to have more IS than OS and green dots for an attempt to have more OS than IS. If there had been no deviation from chance, the red bell curve and the green bell curve would be directly on top of the bell curve of chance. Miraculously, that is not what they saw. The two different intentions had in fact shifted the bell curves! These participants—ordinary, everyday people—had been able to influence the outcome of a completely random machine.

Jahn and Dunne went on to collect data for the next twenty-five years, amassing what became the largest database of studies on intention. The findings consistently showed that when the participant willed the machine to behave in a certain way, he or she would influence it a significant percentage of the time.

(Note: For an in-depth look at the science behind intention, I highly recommend Lynn McTaggart's books *The Field: The Quest for the Secret Force of the Universe* and *The Intention Experiment: Using Your Thoughts to Change Your Life and the World*, which are listed in the Resource section.)

What Does This Have to Do with Negative Body Obsession?

Let's extrapolate these findings and apply them to the context of Negative Body Obsession, and any other negative thoughts, beliefs, and feelings, for that matter. If you truly want to live a life free of NBO, you can create it. You can create a world where you love your body and love your life. The key is to first intend it, and then follow the steps outlined in this book.

Just as those research participants influenced the outcome of a random machine by thinking a certain way, so can you effect change in your life by using the power of intention.

How to Set an Intention

I've explained the concept of this powerful field of intention that operates 24-7, making the universe what it is at any given moment. So how do you actualize your own intention? How do you connect with the field so it orchestrates the fulfillment of your desire?

1. Sit in a quiet place and take a few deep, grounding breaths.
2. Think about what you truly want in your life. What would make you happy? What would satisfy your heart's desire? Imagine the particular intention you want to create.
3. Write your intentions down on a piece of paper.
4. Read through your intentions regularly, particularly before meditation (we will cover this in detail in Step 3).

"Well, that is easy enough," you might be saying to yourself. "My intention is to be thin. Permanently. My intention is to eat whatever I want and not gain weight." "I have had these desires for years," you might protest. "Why haven't I achieved them yet?" There are many possible reasons why you have not been able to actualize your intentions—

we'll talk more about those in Step 1. Throughout this book, you will learn how to break free from whatever has been limiting you. First let's explore how to create successful intentions from the get-go.

Criteria of a Successful Intention

To be successful, your intention must:

- Affirm your self-worth and your intrinsic goodness, value, and beauty (it cannot critique, condemn, and chastise part of who you are).
- Originate from a place of acceptance and love of who you are, not a place of rejection and inadequacy.
- Be based on your inherent beauty, goodness, and strength, rather than based on a fear that you are not as beautiful as you should be.

All of these elements are in direct opposition to NBO and the lies it has told you. If you have been unsuccessful in fulfilling intentions in the past, it is likely that one or more of the above elements were missing. Fortunately, you will learn how to improve your intentions in the next chapter.

Ultimately, in order to successfully manifest your intentions, you want to align yourself with the field of intention. You do this by affirming, fundamentally, that you are inherently beautiful, lovable, and worthwhile. You do this through relinquishing your need to control, by surrendering your attachment to the outcome.

Letting Go of Your Intention

Once your intention is set, you need to release it. In his book *The Seven Spiritual Laws of Success*, Deepak Chopra outlines seven laws that nature uses to create everything in material existence. You can use these same laws to create your heart's desires.

One law in particular applies here: the Law of Detachment. (In order to manifest your dreams and desires, it is best to adhere to all the laws, but I'll just discuss this one here.)

According to the Law of Detachment, in order to manifest your dreams and desires, you must first relinquish your attachment to them. This does *not* mean that you necessarily lose your desire or your passion for them. Quite the contrary; you can be unequivocally clear with your intention, but still release your attachment to the result. This means letting go of the intense neediness, cling- ing, and obsessing about getting what you want when you want it. When you set an intention fueled by passion and purpose, and yet are able to let go of attachment to the results, you can truly begin to change, grow, and develop into the person you wish to become, and acquire whatever things you wish to have.

Know that *you have the power to create a beautiful world.*

This concept is best demonstrated in nature. Everything in nature grows and develops in rhythm and harmony, synchronized with the sea- sons. Imagine an acorn that said, "I want to become an oak tree right now; I need to be a full-grown oak tree immediately. I absolutely need to become a tall, beautiful, strong oak tree right now." Assume for a moment that it could insist its way into instantly becoming an oak tree. It might be tall and beautiful for a moment, but it would not have the requisite roots in place to allow it to survive through rugged winters and sun-parched summers. It would soon fall over, wither, and die.

Instead, imagine this same little acorn, full of the same passion and conviction. The desire to become an oak tree is not the problem. Even the intense and burning desire is not a problem. It is the demanding, obsessive, needy quality of desire that creates problems. It is the insistence that the fulfillment of its desires occur on its time frame that creates difficulty.

Now imagine instead that this little acorn took its passion and desire and planted them deep into its heart and soul. It did whatever it could to make sure it was in the right soil, with good sunlight and water, and symbiotic plants around it. Then it let go and trusted that the very energy that intended it to become an oak tree (which knew it would become an oak tree before it even existed) would eventually fulfill its burning desire to become a huge and powerful oak tree.

The little acorn released its intention, and detached from the outcome, knowing that the force that created many beautiful and glorious oak trees would also fulfill its dreams when the season was right. And before the little acorn even realized it, it became a powerful, beautiful, and glorious oak.

You can create a world where you feel great *in* and *about your body* and *your life*.

This is the way that you must approach your intention to get maximum results. Once you identify your deep and burning desires, you must plant them in your heart and in your soul. You must do everything you can to create an environment in which they can be nurtured. You must release your attachment, your neediness, and your clinging to the result. Instead, trust that the universal force of intention, which is always on time, will fulfill your desires when the time is right.

What Can Intention Do for You?

When you create a proper intention and then align yourself with its all-pervading field, you harness its inherent power to create what you

What Needs to Change?

Take a moment to reflect on what in your life is marked by strain, discomfort, and frustration. What in your life is not working the way you want it to? What in your life are you pushing against? As you read through the next chapter, keep this list with you. You will discover some of what might be preventing you from fulfilling your intentions. Throughout this book, you will learn how to step into the field of intention, remove resistance, and fulfill your desires with more ease and less effort.

want in your life, including being completely free from Negative Body Obsession and creating a body that you feel great in and about.

Beyond freeing you from NBO, intention can also help you in other areas of your life. In fact, everything we discuss in this book applies not only to NBO but to *any* negative thought, feeling, or belief you have about yourself. Don't underestimate the importance of intention. When you learn to treat yourself with love and acceptance, your intentions can bring harmony into disharmony, order into chaos, and transform any mess into a success. That's a powerful force.

Onward!

I realize I've given you a lot to digest in this chapter. If it's unfamiliar territory, don't be intimidated. Living from the field of intention will require a shift, but one that will ultimately bring you unlimited peace, joy, and abundance. Let's start the process with Step 1.

Points to Remember

- Intention is a field that creates and animates everything in existence.
- You have the power to influence your reality
- You can create intentions that harness the power of this field to create what you want in life.
- When you form an intention that comes from a place of acceptance and love, you can create anything that you desire and live the life of your dreams.

Part II

The Five Steps
to Freedom

CHAPTER SIX

Step 1:
Set a Powerful Intention

Now that you understand what intentions are and how powerful they can be, you can develop one (or more) that will allow you to overcome NBO and create the relationship with food and your body that you desire. Once you have set your intentions (see the exercise on the next page), the rest of the book will simply help you fulfill them.

How NBO Disempowers Intentions

Let's take a look at how Negative Body Obsession renders your intentions ineffective. Yes, NBO (and other limiting thoughts, beliefs, and behaviors) disempowers and deactivates the power of intention. Let me explain how by telling you a story about my own experience with creating intentions.

When I was first introduced to the idea that I could realize my dreams and desires, I was energized and enlivened by the hope that my life could move in the direction I wanted it to go. Being an eager student, I wrote my intentions down on a piece of paper to aid in their manifestation, as you are about to.

Write Down Your Intentions

What is your intention in reading this book? What would you like to gain from it?

You may have *many* things that you want to change; that's fine. Start by writing down a list of your desires. Clarity is not essential at this point. They can be short and sweet. Just look quietly into your heart and ask: If I could have anything, what would it be? What is the deepest longing in my heart and soul? What is the pain that I want to heal? What is the pleasure I want to experience?

There are no limits to how many desires you might have. Whatever your specific intention or intentions surrounding food and your body, write them down on a piece of paper. Here are some ideas:

- I want better health.
- I want a stronger, more fit body.
- I want relaxation.
- I want to feel loved.
- I want greater intimacy.
- I want to live at peace with myself and with others.
- I want to be happy.
- I want to be beautiful.

Here is what my list looked like:

- I AM THIN, I AM THIN, I AM THIN, I AM THIN, I AM THIN, I AM THIN, I AM THIN, I AM THIN, I AM THIN, I AM THIN, I AM THIN, I AM THIN, I AM THIN, I AM THIN, I AM THIN, I AM THIN, I AM THIN, I AM THIN, I AM THIN.
- I live in a beautiful country setting.
- I have deep and enriching friendships.
- I have perfect health.
- I have a beautiful love relationship.

A little emphatic, don't you think? When I wrote them, I was actually already very thin, weighing around 105 pounds on my 5'3" frame. But:

- I was chronically afraid that I might gain weight.
- My identity was still determined, in my mind, by how much I weighed and how I looked.
- I unconsciously believed that my self-worth, my success, and my lovability were determined by my being thin.

For these reasons, there was a desperate, grasping quality to my intention. I needed my desire to be fulfilled so that I could accept and approve of myself.

In the six months after I wrote that list of desires, I gained 30 pounds, lost 80 percent of my flexibility, my physical health deteriorated, and I fell into a nine-month-long intense and practically suicidal depression. So much for the power of intention, right?

Wrong. The problem was not with intention. The problem was with how I was using intention and what I was doing to disempower it. My NBO limited the amount of greatness I could experience; it limited my ability to both envision and create the life of my dreams.

I share this story to demonstrate how NBO disempowers intention. Here are some of the main ways that NBO can block your ability to connect with the field of intention and manifest your desires:

1. NBO ties your self-worth to a specific outcome. This makes it difficult, if not impossible, to detach from the results.
2. NBO causes you to reject or deny your inherent beauty, goodness, and strength.
3. NBO affects the quality of your intention because it comes from a place of desperation rather than a place of love.
4. NBO highlights your fears instead of your trust and self-love.
5. NBO makes it difficult to accept the present (and love yourself as you are right now).

You're probably noticing how these factors are in conflict with the criteria of a successful intention you read about on page 42. Let's look at each of them in more detail.

NBO Forces Your Self-Worth to Be Determined by an Outcome

When you set your intentions, did you imply in any of them that your self-worth is determined by the outcome of your intention?

Ask yourself

WHAT RESULTS OR CONDITIONS IN YOUR LIFE DO YOU USE TO DETERMINE YOUR SELF-WORTH? Relying on an outcome disempowers your intention because when you let your self-worth be determined by a specific result, you are denying the fact that you are inherently beautiful, lovable, and worthwhile *exactly as you are, right here and right now.* You are deciding that you are only worthy of greatness if you look a certain way or achieve a certain thing. Yet for your intention to succeed, you must love yourself exactly as you are right now. If you don't, you are in direct opposition to the energy that you want to tap into in order to turn your intentions into reality.

Whether your self-worth is determined by your body size, your bank account size, or by anything else in your life, the principle remains the same: when you make your self-worth dependent on a particular outcome, you deny part of yourself and therefore weaken your connection to intention and your ability to manifest greatness in your own life. Instead, embrace all of yourself with love.

Intention is always-providing.

NBO Causes You to Deny and Reject Yourself

Do the intentions you wrote down implicitly deny or reject part of who you are?

This challenge to intention shows up whenever we prefer that a part of ourselves did not exist. If you are thin and obsessed with maintaining a low body weight, you may deny the part of you that wants to overeat and be out of control. If you tend to binge regularly and have less control, you may deny the part of yourself that wants to exert control. You might deny the part of yourself that is vain and worried about other people's opinions. Or you may deny that part of yourself that could care less what anyone thinks. We are all full of these contradictions—peace comes from learning to reconcile the seemingly oppositional forces within us.

Ask yourself

WHAT PARTS OF YOURSELF DO YOU DENY OR REJECT, WISHING THEY WOULD JUST GO AWAY? Rejecting parts of yourself disempowers your intention because you create a negative counterforce that stymies your efforts. Dr. Wayne Dyer says it beautifully in *The Power of Intention*: "You cannot attract attractiveness into your life by hating anything about what you've allowed yourself to become . . . hatred creates a counter-force of hatred that disempowers your efforts." When you deny part of who you are, you deny your totality and your ultimate beauty, and that takes away your power to manifest your intentions.

Remember: to strengthen your intention, you must align yourself with the field of intention. This field is by its nature all-inclusive, so if you deny parts of yourself, you are not being all-inclusive. However, the field is also all-accepting. If it is everywhere and accepts everything, to deny something would mean that the field of intention was not there, which is impossible because it is everywhere.

Likewise, you must become all-accepting, and this begins first and foremost with yourself. You must form intentions from a place of acceptance, instead of from a place of rejection.

Truly Accepting Yourself

The concept of accepting yourself wholeheartedly may be a difficult one to visualize at this point in your struggle with NBO. Consider this metaphor to help you envision it.

Imagine for a moment that you are a budding rose, not quite in full bloom. One day, you look across the garden and see a tulip. "Oh my gosh," you squeal, "I want to be a tulip!" You look longingly across the flowerbed, yearning to be as stunning as the tulip. You begin to look back at yourself with disdain and eventually disgust. "I am just a rose," you whimper. "I have too many petals; I'm not as slim as a tulip."

Then the idea occurs to you: what if I could become a tulip? "If I was a tulip, I would be beautiful. All the flowers would want to spend time with me, and I would be a huge success." So you try to fashion yourself into a tulip. You pluck and dye your petals, you fertilize, and you change your root system, only to find after endless effort and force, you are still a rose. Only now you are exhausted, overwhelmed, and still dissatisfied with the fact that you are a rose.

It is only when you accept that you are a rose that your true beauty begins to emerge. If you intend to be a tulip, whether this is fully conscious or not, you will be denying the fact that you are a rose. Your intentions will be thwarted because you are acting at odds with the universe and the very energy of intention that you want to connect with.

You can guess the moral of this story: accept your rose-ness. Accept whatever type of rose you are, whatever changes you have made or not made; it doesn't matter. Reclaim any rejected parts of yourself. Then you can set your intention to become the most beautiful, radiant, generous, and glorious rose you can be.

NBO Affects the Quality of Your Intention

By quality of intention here, I do not mean the intention itself is good or bad. Rather, what is the emotion or energy surrounding the intention? Specifically, is there a quality of clinging, neediness, or obsession to your intention?

Ask yourself

DO YOU FEEL AN INTENSE NEED THAT THINGS WORK OUT THE WAY YOU WANT THEM TO? If you desperately need your intention to manifest in a particular way immediately, you are once again at odds with the creative energy of the universe. Instead of trusting that you have access to the power of intention, you attempt to control the outcome and cling to the results. The most powerful intentions come from trusting the process and letting the universe handle the details. When you let go of needing and clinging to a particular timeframe, you let intention do its work and carry you to your desired outcome.

NBO Highlights Your Fears Instead of Your Trust

Ask yourself

IS YOUR INTENTION BASED ON FEAR OR ON TRUST? This question is simply a different way of exploring what we have already been discussing. Does your intention reflect a belief in your own inherent goodness, beauty, and strength? Or does it reflect the assumption that you are not quite good enough the way you are, that if just a few things would change, then you would be great or at least acceptable?

Ask yourself

ARE YOU INTENSELY AFRAID OF NOT GETTING WHAT YOU WANT ACCORDING TO YOUR SCHEDULE? Creating an intention from a place of fear disempowers the intention because your negative feelings beget negative results. Remember, your intention manifests when you tap into and become like the Source of intention. This source is all-inclusive, all-accepting, and always on time. It is also always-providing, so it gives you what you need to achieve maximum growth and development.

Whether you choose to *experience* life as always-providing is an entirely different matter. When you experience life as always giving you what you need, your intentions will have maximum power. On the other hand, when you choose to experience life as a haphazard series of random events that sometimes work out in your favor and sometimes don't, your intentions will be weakened. When you believe you are unable to get what you want in life, you create a reality of lack and frustration, which further separates you from the power of intention.

On the other hand, when you experience life as always providing exactly what you need, in exactly the right amount, at exactly the right time, a couple of things happen:

1. First, you align yourself with the universal power of intention, which is by nature always-providing. You become more like it in your thoughts, actions, and behaviors. This solidifies your connection to it and therefore your ability to use it to influence the direction of your life.
2. Second, you begin to experience trust. You know that life is always providing exactly what you need, even if nothing seems to be going your way. You begin to trust in the process of life, including your

own creative potential. You begin to realize that you have the power, the ability, and the grace to transform whatever you encounter for the better. You learn that you can transform setbacks into advances, challenges into solutions, and adversity into opportunity.

When these two forces take hold, your mindset will change. Instead of wallowing in the anger and frustration of life not working out the way you want it to, you begin to look for evidence that life is providing exactly what you need. You're alert to any opportunities to improve your behavior or to develop a more useful path of action. You develop more energy, more vitality, more enthusiasm, more creativity, and more love, which you can use to improve your own life as well as the lives of everyone around you.

Intention is all-inclusive.

Being Afraid Is Not the Same Thing

Realize that you may very well feel fear, anxiety, and insecurity as you begin to challenge the assumptions and beliefs that you had constructed to keep you safe up to this point. A powerful intention may invoke fear because it is outside your comfort zone. This is a very different phenomenon, however, from an intention being based on fear. Here is an example to illustrate the point:

I was discussing intentions with one of my coaching clients, Linda, a fifty-four-year-old single woman who had been underweight for a number of years. Although she was no longer acutely anorexic, she had been suffering from a number of health issues because of her low body weight.

When we first started working together, she began developing a vision for her life. She wanted to improve her health, and she wanted to develop a beautiful body. She believed that she was too skinny, but when I suggested the intention of developing a healthy relationship with food and her body, she was gripped with fear. Why? A healthy relationship with food and her body implied that her body had a voice. She had spent years constructing her safety and security around controlling her body.

Although she was afraid, her intention of creating a healthy relationship with food and her body was *not* based on fear. It was based on the fundamental belief that health and peace are possible for each and every one of us. Her intention, therefore, was based on trust. Her *response* to this intention, however, evoked fear because it challenged the self-limiting beliefs that were currently keeping her trapped in suffering.

You must learn to differentiate between an intention based on fear and a trust-based intention that evokes fear because you still doubt your own magnificence and creative ability. As you are able to base your intentions increasingly on trust, your ability to manifest your intentions will grow.

NBO Makes It Difficult to Accept the Present

When you set your intentions, are you able to accept the way you are right now?

When struggling with Negative Body Obsession, this may very well be the most important point regarding intention, and the most challenging. If you dislike your body, the most difficult thing to do is accept the present. You are bothered by how your body looks, whether overweight, underweight, or average. You have been told by society that if you want to change your body, you must do certain things. You must eat less, exercise more; lift weights, do more sit-ups. You run around literally and figuratively, frantically trying to change.

The problem is that you have never accepted your body as it is, at this moment. The resistance you have toward your body—and anything else in your life—is what prevents you from making the changes you want and fulfilling your intention.

Ask yourself

WHAT ARE YOU FIGHTING AGAINST IN YOUR LIFE RIGHT NOW? Your lack of acceptance of the present moment adversely impacts your intentions for a number of reasons:

1. **It puts you in opposition to the energy of the universe.** The present moment is what it is. You can change anything in the next moment, but this moment is undeniably what it is. Remember, you are not an isolated entity, so the present moment is not just a result of your choices, but of the choices of others throughout the world and throughout all time. When you fight against the present moment and you refuse to accept it, you are fighting against the entire universe. Needless to say, that's a losing battle!

2. **It puts you in opposition to yourself.** You are exactly who you are because of whatever choices you have made, for whatever reasons. You are inherently beautiful, lovable, and worthwhile simply because you exist, regardless of anything else in your life. When you fight against the present moment and against yourself, you reject your power and weaken your connection to the power of intention.

3. **You drain important energy away from your intention.** When you are in opposition to something, you are fighting it. Fighting takes a tremendous amount of energy and effort. Rather than focusing single-mindedly on your intention, you become sidetracked by ruminating on what you dislike or what you wish were different. Instead, you must completely accept the present moment, create an intention that affects the future, and then gently move in that direction.

4. **It makes you attract negativity.** Realize that you attract what you think about most of the time. If you are thinking and acting in resistance to the present moment, you will stay stuck, living in opposition and frustration. On the other hand, when you accept the present moment, you will quiet your mental chatter and have more ability to focus and direct your thinking, and therefore your life.

5. **You are limiting your power as a creator.** You want to own and actualize your creative power. When you resist the present moment, you deny your creative power and ability. When you accept the present moment, you release and compound your creative power so that you can more easily and effortlessly create what you desire.

Accepting the Present Does NOT Equal Complacency

In my own struggle with NBO, I was most challenged by the idea of accepting myself as I was at a given moment. Here's how I faced that challenge:

I had always received a great deal of satisfaction from being thin and fit. As already explained, my identity was dependent on having a thin and fit body. When I gained 30 pounds over a three-month period, I plummeted into a severe and debilitating depression. During this time, my whole sense of identity and self-worth was destroyed. I needed to confront the very strong belief that if I wasn't thin and fit, I simply wasn't successful. I believed that I wasn't worthwhile, that I was a failure. If you live with NBO, you know how real and debilitating these thoughts and beliefs can appear.

I hated myself for failing; I hated my body for not doing what I wanted. I was angry, frustrated, agonizing, and quite literally wanted to die. It was in that moment of my deepest and darkest despair that I realized: I must accept myself exactly how I am. I must. I didn't know how; I didn't want to, but I knew that I had to find my intrinsic value and self-worth in that moment, regardless of what was happening.

You must realize that *accepting the present does not mean you will not or cannot change*. In fact, that is absolutely impossible because everything is constantly changing. It is simply not possible for you to remain the same, regardless of how much you want to. The real questions are "How are you changing?" and "In what direction are you moving?"

Intention is *without* limitation.

Accepting the present is not about complacency. As I began to accept the present moment, I asked: How can I use my pain to help others? I knew I had to do something; I had to get out and make connections with people, even though I felt embarrassed, unworthy, and unlovable.

This shift, from fighting vehemently against the present moment and my current situation, to accepting it and myself unconditionally, set in motion events that have changed my life. I have constructed a rewarding career; have the honor of writing this book to share with you; and consistently make connections with amazing, enthusiastic, and supportive people who are also passionate about making a difference in the world. I enjoy great health and vitality. When I accepted the present and intended the future, I relaxed, knowing that everything was being orchestrated and accomplished by the creative power of the universe.

Accept the Present, but Continually Evolve

The field of intention is always-evolving. By connecting with intention, you can also become always-evolving. You can continue to learn, grow, and develop at every phase of your life. You can learn how to improve your mind and your body, connect with your spirit, and improve your relationships. You can ensure that the changes you are experiencing are the most evolutionary ones for you, designed to move you from where you are to where you want to be.

The way to maximize your evolution is through accepting the present moment, accepting yourself, accepting your world, and intending the future. This is how you will harness the power to move you in the direction you want to go. When you connect with intention and are all-accepting, you can make sure you are always-evolving toward continued happiness.

Hint: You Already Are What You Want to Be

Reframing intentions in terms of "having" is certainly effective and will yield benefits for the reasons I just mentioned. I want to explore another reason for focusing on "being," however.

In truth, you already are that which you desire. Your only job is to discover and experience it. The deeper your knowing and your experience of who you really are, the greater your ability to manifest your dreams and desires. The shift is from wanting, to having, to being.

Reframing Your Intentions

I'm guessing that after reading that last section, you realized that some of your intentions need to be revised. That's okay—it's all part of the process. As a first step in the revision process, let's reframe your intentions so they come from a place of love and acceptance instead of desperation.

We can do that with one simple change. Take your list and replace the words "I want" with the words "I am." Here are some examples:

- I am perfect health.
- I am strong.
- I am fit.
- I am peaceful.
- I am calm.
- I am relaxed.
- I am love.
- I am intimacy.
- I am happy.
- I am calm.
- I am secure.
- I am beauty.

The language you use regarding your intentions is important. According to some teachers, if you consistently say "I want," you will remain in state of perpetual wanting. But if you say "I have perfect health," "I have strength," etc., you can move to a state of having instead. Here's another suggestion: couple the intention with an emotion to add fuel and energy. An example is "I feel so happy and energetic in my fit, strong, agile body." This can help to motivate and energize you, aligning you with what you want to create.

You're probably thinking: "But Sarah, I'm 50 pounds overweight! How can I say I AM thin just because I want to be that way?" Here's how to look at this situation. If you are 50 pounds overweight, saying "I AM THIN" is not going to magically make you thin. What's important, however, is the shift in consciousness from a small sense of self to an understanding that you are the very power that creates worlds. You are the unbounded, pure potential that can manifest whatever you desire. When you begin to live from this place, you have a much greater chance of losing the 50 pounds that you might want to lose.

Here's how the process works:

1. When you want something, you're in this state of *wanting* (duh). This phase is useful because it's when you discover your dreams and aspirations. If you stay in this state of wanting, however, they will remain dreams and aspirations and will not as readily become part of your reality.
2. When you shift to *having*, you can acquire many great things. That's great, right? Yes, but consider this: whatever you have, you can also lose. Anything material can be taken from you.
3. When you shift to *being*, however, you shift to the eternal and unbounded realm where every desire is already fulfilled. You are the creator and the experience; you are the artist and the artwork. You are your dreams and your desires, and you are so much more. From this place, there is no such thing as lack, and nothing can ever be lost. This is where you want to be!

Questions to Ask Yourself

Now that you know the challenges that NBO has created for you, ask yourself the following questions to help you ensure that your intentions have maximum power.

Do You Believe You Deserve It?

Do you believe that you deserve to receive what you want in life?

Many of the people I work with who struggle with NBO don't believe that they deserve to receive what they want. They don't think they deserve to lose weight, enjoy their body, experience love, or whatever else they desire.

*A*s*k* yourself

WHAT DO YOU NOT ASK FOR BECAUSE YOU DON'T THINK YOU DESERVE IT? It is not a matter of believing that you deserve it because you are better than anyone else, or that you deserve it more than anyone else. It is not a matter of deserving it because you are lucky or have done everything perfectly in your life. You deserve it; I deserve it; and anyone else deserves it as well.

Life with NBO = Scarcity and Depravity

Most of us struggling with NBO are trained to think in terms of limitation and scarcity. We think that if we are entitled to something, if we deserve something, then we are somehow taking away from someone else. We don't want to be perceived of as selfish and demanding, so we limit ourselves and what we think we can and should receive.

Learn to realize the difference between entitlement and abundance. *Entitlement* is the voice of the ego, demanding that life provide you with exactly what you want, when you want it. It is a voice that implies you are more deserving than someone else.

Abundance, on the other hand, is the quiet reality that we all deserve and most people sell themselves short of receiving. There is enough for everyone. We all deserve everything, all the time. We all deserve goodness, beauty, grace, and power. We deserve a life free from suffering. We deserve a life of love and abundance.

Life Without NBO = Abundance and Sharing

When you connect with the power of intention, you discover that it is always-abundant, giving without limitation to everyone and everything. It is important, however, to focus on deserving things that are mutually beneficial for everyone, and not trying to get something that will knowingly harm anyone else in any way.

There are a few things, of course, that you never deserve, such as pain, agony, or suffering. You never deserve to feel pain; you never deserve to be hurt or abused in any way. You also never deserve to cause pain or harm to anyone else. Yes, you might experience pain and suffering, but you don't deserve it.

The more you have, the more you can share. If you are fit, help someone else become fit. If you are strong, help someone else become strong. If you are beautiful, help someone else become beautiful. If you are healthy, help someone else become healthy. If you have love, help someone else experience love. If you have money, help someone else acquire money.

Whatever you have you can give away, but if you don't have it, you can't give it. If you feel tired, stressed, fat, ugly, and depressed, how much can you impact the world? On the other hand, if you feel strong, energetic, vibrant, powerful, and beautiful, how much can you impact the world? How much you can give is in direct proportion to how much you have, and this applies to absolutely everything in your life.

One concern that I hear from women in particular is: "If I am attractive, other women will be jealous." This same concern can be expressed regarding wealth, relationships, or anything else that we say, have, or do. This is an outdated mindset that is based on a model of scarcity instead of abundance. The reason other people are jealous is because they want what you have. You are a reflection to them of their potential. If their potential is not being manifest, they feel jealous. They see their greatness in you, and want to achieve it as well.

We have all achieved some success and some greatness in our lives. When you share it or give it away, you will not only help the recipient; the selflessness will increase whatever you have. You will gain more of everything and begin to experience even more love and abundance. We are all on this journey of life together. Our desires and dreams are more similar than they are different. When we give what we have, we replace limitation with abundance, solidifying our connection to the always-abundant power of intention.

Do You Think It's Possible?

What are you not trying for because you think it is impossible?

Many of us never dare to dream because we are afraid it is impossible. You may be worried that you cannot achieve what you want, that it is simply not possible. Maybe it is possible for someone else, but not for you. You remind yourself that you have failed in the past, so it must be impossible in the future.

Diana's Story

Take, for example, Diana, one of my *Beautiful Life* e-zine subscribers (sign up for your free subscription at *www.sarahmaria.com*). She's forty years old, 5'4" tall, and weighs 285 pounds. She is increasingly inactive physically because of aches and pains. Her weight has gone up and down her entire life. She is heavier now than she has ever been. She is often miserable and filled with self-hatred. She takes an antidepressant to help dull the edge of her discontent. She says that if she loved herself more she would be less destructive toward her body.

I asked her what she thought prevented her from making changes in her life. What was limiting her from achieving the health, happiness, love, and fulfillment that she deserved? Her answer: "I tell myself that it is not possible. I have gained and lost weight so many times, over so many years, why should I believe it can be any different? I convince myself that I can't do it, so I never have the opportunity to fail."

Do her thoughts sound familiar?

Ask yourself

WHAT ARE YOU NOT TRYING TO BE, DO, OR HAVE BECAUSE YOU ARE AFRAID YOU WILL NOT SUCCEED? Remember, the nature of intention is that it is without limitation. It is boundless, timeless, pure potential. In Diana's case, she assumed that because she had not accomplished her goals in the past, she could not accomplish them in the future. She erroneously concluded that her goals were unachievable and impossible. There are many reasons why Diana didn't achieve her goals, just as there are many reasons you might not have achieved your goals in the past. But the reason is not that the goals were inherently impossible.

Here are some likely reasons you may have failed in the past:

1. **You probably did not have the right information to lead you to the fulfillment of your goal.** In the area of weight loss, new research yields a constant stream of new information about how best to lose weight. Perhaps some tips or techniques that are available to you now weren't available then. In Diana's case, although she was able to lose weight temporarily, she was not making the lifestyle changes—physical, emotional, mental, and spiritual—to help her achieve her goals.

2. **Perhaps part of you did not feel you deserved it, or wasn't sure you even really wanted it.** There are many reasons that we unwittingly sabotage our efforts.

3. **Maybe you didn't have the support you needed to fulfill your desire.** Successful achievement of any goal requires tremendous support. Following the steps is in this book will help you get the support you need.

Assess What You Have Now

Look at your own life. Instead of assuming that something is impossible, look specifically at what prevented you from getting the result you wanted in the past. Often new information, a new book, a coach, a mentor, a teacher, or an "accountability partner" (a friend or colleague—someone whom you can check in with and who can be sure you're doing what you said you'd do) can make all the difference in the world, whatever your dream, goal, or aspiration.

Think Big

Realize that intention is without limitation. Look at your life and your world from this place of limitless abundance. The very nature of intention is unlimited. Use your dreams to transcend the ordinary and opt instead for the extraordinary and to create the mythical life that you are worthy of living.

Every great invention has been conceived because people were willing to live outside the limits that confine most people. Where would travel be if the Wright brothers contemplated the impossibility of their dream? Where would health be if Louis Pasteur believed illnesses that killed people could not be prevented or cured? Where would art be if Picasso, Van Gogh, and Michelangelo believed they could not achieve something extraordinary? Where would technology be if scientists thought the only existence was what we perceive through our five senses?

You get the point—dream big!

Are You Prepared to Show Perseverance to Set This Intention?

You may not achieve something your first try, or your second, or your third. Almost every great accomplishment has been achieved through a series of perceived failures. Thomas Edison tried more than 10,000 experiments before he finally produced a light bulb. He insisted that these were not failures; he simply discovered 10,000 ways that a light bulb didn't work, all of which led to the one way that it did work.

So-called failures are simply learning opportunities so you can do better the next time you try. If you are not where you want to be in your life, find people who have accomplished what you want to accomplish, or have done something similar to what you want to do. Study them, learn from them, and you will discover what you need to know to fulfill your dreams. There is a miraculous and abundant world just waiting to be experienced.

Sorting Out Your Feelings

You might very well find yourself in conflict regarding your intentions. You may feel excited and motivated one moment and fearful and helpless the next.

Take the example of Shira, one of my subscribers, a twenty-nine-year-old from an upper-middle-class American family. She had a pleasant upbringing with loving parents and describes herself as well educated and attractive. She never had a problem with her weight until she lived abroad during her sophomore year in high school. She went on a cruise to various parts of the world, and while she was traveling she gained some weight. When she returned home, her family and her boyfriend commented on her weight gain. She was mortified. She was embarrassed and ashamed. Although she lost the weight, a struggle began. She developed bulimia in an attempt to keep her weight down. Her struggle was ongoing but hidden from everyone. No one knew about her fight with her body, but it was something that plagued her constantly.

Shira learned about my work and told me of her struggles. She sent me an e-mail after having a heart-wrenching experience. She visited the DMV to renew her driver's license and the woman at the counter inquired if she was pregnant. She wrote:

> After the lady made the comment, I had this huge breakdown—in the car with my father!!—and I was just hysterically crying over the eight years of my life that I've spent dwelling on NBO. I haven't let go like that in years, maybe ever.

. . . There are two sides of me—one that is in sync with what you wrote {that she is beautiful and can never not be beautiful}, and the other that tells me all I need to do is lose weight and then everything will be better. For so long now I have been identified with the first side, but after this week, I feel more identified with the other. But mostly I believe what you said in the end: "Trust that your body will find its own healthy weight in its own time and that you will develop a healthy relationship to food and your body." Also: "her image of you is a projection of her own consciousness"—how true! Just the day before I was weighed at the doctor's office and was feeling awful because of that. And the very next morning she made that comment . . .

I am feeling positive today, and will read your e-mail over and over, maybe I'll print out a copy to carry with me!

There was nothing wrong with Shira wanting to achieve fitness and health, beauty and strength. The problem occurred when she criticized and condemned parts of herself for her perceived imperfections. There is nothing wrong with the two sides within Shira or within any of us. It is perfectly okay to desire health, beauty, and vitality. It is also okay to recognize your inherent beauty as it is now. Simply allow any apparent paradoxes or contradictions to be what they are, gently favoring that which affirms your intrinsic beauty, goodness, and value.

Moving On

The following chapters will give you the tools and techniques you need to learn how to accept yourself. From this place of pure acceptance and pure love, you can fulfill your dreams and desires.

If you're not in a place yet to accept yourself, don't judge or critique that part of you that says "I just want to be thin" or "If only I had the body that I had back then" (or however your particular story line

Finalize Your Intentions

Your intentions have probably come a long way from the exercise at the beginning of this chapter! Now is the time to review each of them again to be sure they meet the principles of successful intentions. For each of your intentions, ask yourself the following question: Is this intention affirming my inherent goodness, beauty, value, and self-worth? Or is it critiquing, condemning, and chastising part of who I am?

When you feel ready to step out of the struggle and into the peace, fashion your desires into intentions that affirm your goodness, beauty, value, and self-worth exactly as you are, in this moment. The more you are able to accept yourself fully and completely, the greater your ability to move your life in the direction that you want it to go.

sounds). This entire book is about helping you change your story into one that will be more productive and beneficial. This new story will include looking and feeling great, so don't think that you have to settle for anything. For now, list your intentions, asking yourself if they affirm that you are deserving of all great love, beauty, and affection.

Accept the present, *intend* the future.

Points to Remember

- Be aware of the ways NBO, and other negative thoughts, beliefs, and behaviors, weaken your connection to the power of intention by:

  1. Letting your self-worth be determined by the outcome
  2. Denying and rejecting part of who you are

3. Having the qualities of clinging, neediness, and obsession surrounding your intention

4. Basing your intentions on fear instead of trust

5. Refusing to accept the present moment

- When you create intentions, ask yourself:

  1. Do I believe that I deserve it?
  2. Do I believe that it is possible?

- For maximum effectiveness, become like the field of intention in all of your thoughts, words, and deeds:

  1. Become all-inclusive, loving every part of yourself, affirming your inherent beauty, goodness, value, and self-worth.
  2. Become all-accepting, honoring all of yourself in your beautiful uniqueness.
  3. Rest in the peace of knowing that your intentions will manifest when the time is right.
  4. Acknowledge the ways that life is always-providing, giving you exactly what you need, right on schedule.
  5. Realize yourself as always-evolving, as you accept the present and intend the future.
  6. Focus on being always-abundant, attracting all the greatness you deserve.
  7. Live without limitation, knowing that at your essence you are pure, unbounded potential.

- The power of intention is the power of love. If you want your inten-
tions to yield maximum results, create them always to affirm your greatness, beauty, and glory.

CHAPTER SEVEN

Step 2: Identify and Detach from Your Negative Body Thoughts

If you struggle with some form of Negative Body Obsession, you are all too familiar with the thoughts that create your suffering. What you may not realize is that these thoughts are just that—simply thoughts. *You* give them the power to control your health, your happiness, and your life by listening to them unequivocally and without question. Most of us travel through life never realizing that we can ignore our thoughts! Instead, we often believe that our thoughts define us.

Separate Yourself from Your Thoughts

Where do we go wrong? First, we take our thoughts very seriously. We either identify completely with them or, at the very least, take responsibility for having them. Second, we are caught in a vicious cycle of constantly reacting to our thoughts and responding compulsively, obeying the commands of a schizophrenic drill sergeant with no direction.

Jennifer's Story

Take, for example, one of my subscribers, Jennifer. She's in her forties, and weighing almost 300 pounds, is considered obese. Here is her story that she shared with me:

I have been fat my entire life. I always joked that I was born as a blob of fat with eyes. My mother was very beautiful and always concerned about her appearance. I knew I would never be able to compete with her in the looks department, so I figured I wouldn't even try. At a very young age, food became a substitute for love and affection. I am currently being medicated for depression. Without medication I begin to think, "I'm useless, worthless, no one will ever miss me if I die," and my self-hatred spirals out of control. I am reticent to have sex because I am repulsed by my own body. If I have ice cream and chips, however, I forget about feeling bad.

I know that if I loved myself more, I wouldn't be so destructive toward my body.

Jennifer basically wrote an entire story about herself, her self-worth, her lovability, and her relationship to food that is dictating, creating, and determining the quality of her life. When she tells herself that she is a blob of fat with eyes, it is no surprise that she faces uncontrollable depression. When she tells herself that she is not beautiful enough to experience sensual pleasure, she cuts herself off from the ability to experience love and affection. The thoughts she has about herself continue to create and influence a painful and negative situation. She has identified with her thoughts; she believes that her thoughts are real and true. This misperception gives her thoughts control over her life and renders her powerless.

The Path to Freedom

It is when we discover that we are not our thoughts, and that we do not have to listen to our thoughts, that the path to freedom begins. Dr. David Simon, medical director of the Chopra Center for Well-being, says it this way: "The best thought you can ever think is the thought that you are not your thoughts." Whoever you are (and we will address that question specifically in the following chapter), know that your thoughts do not define you.

The Origin of Thoughts

So if you are not your thoughts, where do your Negative Body Thoughts come from? The majority of them have most likely come from the people who have influenced you the most. This usually includes our parents or parental surrogates. Our thought patterns were established when we were very young, and our parents played an instrumental role in creating them. Our parents gave us ideas about who we were, what we were capable of, what we were entitled to, and what we were worth. Our thoughts have also been influenced by teachers, siblings, friends, and society at large.

> You *are not* your thoughts; you are *the witness* to your thoughts.

And, sorry to burst your bubble: very few of your Negative Body Thoughts, if any, are original. They have been passed down to you from others. Your parents', teachers', siblings', and friends' thoughts were also not their own, but rather were passed down to them from the people who influenced their lives.

Take Charge of Your Negative Body Thoughts

So: We are not responsible for creating our thoughts, for they are not our own. We can, however, take responsibility over our thoughts. Once you realize that your thoughts are not yours, you can assume some authority over them. You can choose either to listen or not to listen, depending on whether the thought is useful, edifying, enriching, and evolutionary, or destructive, negative, and depleting. If the thought is not uplifting, it is better to dismiss it.

Thoughts are energy and have the ability to influence our psychology and biology in profound ways, either for good or for ill. Thoughts play an integral role in the development of our lives and in the development of our health and well-being, or the lack thereof. When you listen to the thoughts you have been given (by parents, friends, teachers, and society at large) without being aware of them and their influence on you, you most likely will suffer. When, however, you become aware of your thoughts, you can make conscious choices about what thoughts you're going to let grow within your psyche.

Once you identify and proactively detach from the *negative* thoughts, you can begin to cultivate and nurture *positive* thoughts that have the power to utterly transform your life. You can create a new reality for yourself by changing your thoughts. As you change your thoughts, you will change your life.

Imagine what Jennifer's life could look like if she realized that she didn't need to listen to every thought. She could create an entirely different story about herself that would yield completely different results in her life. She could acknowledge the influences that have shaped her up until this point. She could make a choice, however, not to continue to be limited by those beliefs. She could develop a story that would move her in the direction she wants to go. Instead of telling herself that she is fat, ugly, and worthless, she could use every thought, word, and action to affirm her beauty, glory, goodness, and strength. She could use every experience in her life as an opportunity to affirm her self-worth. She would no longer be forced to re-create the same hopeless situation again and again. She could literally change her life by changing her thoughts.

Have you ever stopped to ask: *Where do my thoughts come from?*

More Science to Convince You

I know, I know. You're thinking: "Come on, Sarah Maria! I can't change my life just by thinking different thoughts. It's much more complicated than that." Actually, it's not. But don't take my word for it—read on for a look at the latest research.

How Athletes Prove My Point

Some of the most fascinating studies of how our thoughts impact reality come from sports. Most athletes consistently practice some form of mental rehearsal to improve performance. The athlete imagines the event as if he or she were actually living it in this moment. In her book *The Intention Experiment*, Lynn McTaggart discusses some intriguing examples.

In one study, skiers were wired to special EMG equipment while visualizing skiing down slopes. (EMG stands for electromyography, and it offers a real-time view of the brain's instructions to the body. It records every electrical impulse that is sent from motor neurons to specific muscles in the body to signal a contraction.) The EMG results showed that when ski-

> You have the *power* to transform your brain.

ers mentally rehearsed their downhill runs, the electrical impulses sent to their muscles were *exactly the same* as those they used while actually performing on the slopes. That means that their brains sent exactly the same instructions to the body whether the skiers were thinking about skiing or actually skiing!

You SHOULD Still Exercise, But . . .

Another intriguing study showed that mental intention or focused thoughts can produce actual physiological changes in the body. Research conducted by Guang Yue, an exercise psychologist at the Cleveland Clinic Foundation in Ohio, compared participants (twenty to thirty-five years of age) who went to a gym regularly with those who practiced a visual workout in their minds, while their bodies remained seated in an armchair. Those who went to the gym increased their overall muscle strength by 30 percent. Those who sat in place and visualized weight training increased their overall strength by almost half as much! The researchers conducted a few variations:

- Participants imagined flexing their biceps as hard as they could during daily exercise sessions five days a week. After just a few weeks, they experienced a 13.5 percent increase in muscle size and strength. This benefit remained for three months after the actual mental training had stopped.
- Participants who worked out could achieve 30 percent increases in strength, while those who just imagined themselves doing the training achieved a 16 percent increase.

You no longer need to be a *prisoner* to the voices inside your head.

Although the imagined activity had a smaller magnitude (as I said, you should probably still do the actual exercises), it had a clear mental and physical effect. Other studies have confirmed that thought can influence other areas, including improving health, reducing stress, and lowering blood pressure. See? Science has shown that if you can think or visualize it, you are well on your way to achieving it.

Can't I Just Start "Thinking Positive"?

Sorry, no. Simply thinking positive thoughts is rarely effective because many of us have been living with perpetually negative thought patterns for years.

Here is another nature metaphor for you: It would be like trying to plant beautiful flowers in a bed full of weeds. Why would you do that? The weeds would prevent the flowers from blooming. First you would want to pull out the weeds and till the soil. Then you would plant the flowers and provide appropriate water and sunlight so they would grow with ease.

That is what we are going to do. We are first going to uproot the weeds (the negative thoughts) that are keeping you trapped. Once we have cleared the way, we are going to plant positive thoughts that will begin to take root so that they can grow and transform your life.

The best way to begin this process is for you to discover your current thought patterns. The exercises on the following pages are designed to help you identify and then separate yourself from your habitual thoughts.

Uncovering the "Wizard" in Your Thoughts

What you will discover from the exercise on Identifying Your Negative Thoughts is that your thoughts are extremely repetitive and (again, sorry to burst your bubble) entirely unoriginal. We all have a tendency to take them so seriously, to let them control our lives . . . but upon investigation, we discover they are nothing more than a repetitive, boring, constant recording that got stuck on "repeat" for years.

Think of them being like the Wizard of Oz. He was a little man who controlled people through his supposedly "wondrous" powers. Everyone just accepted the fact that he had magical powers, but upon investigation, they learned he was nothing more than a charlatan. He was orchestrating a grand illusion, a grand delusion (sound familiar?). He was able to do it because no one questioned his authority. It was not until Dorothy challenged the Wizard that the truth was discovered: he was nothing more than a lonely, insecure old man, demanding power in a vain attempt to fuel his ego.

Identify Your Negative Thoughts

Change begins with awareness. You have to become acutely aware of the way you talk to yourself and about yourself. As you notice what you say to yourself, discover how these thoughts, beliefs, and attitudes make you feel and direct your behavior. Our lives are the result of the thoughts we think on an ongoing basis. As we think, so we become.

If you are constantly thinking Negative Body Thoughts, you will adversely impact your body, your health, and your life. We will explore how our thoughts affect our physiology in detail in Step 4, Befriend Your Body, but for now realize that the quality of your thoughts determines the quality of your life. The way you think about yourself will determine:

- The way you feel about yourself
- The quality of your friendships
- The quality of your career
- The quality of your health
- Basically . . . every aspect of your life

You'll begin by figuring out what your negative thoughts are. Purchase a small notebook that can fit in your purse or pocket. For the next two weeks, carry this notebook with you wherever you go. Every time you notice yourself having a Negative Body Thought, write it down. Also write down the negative feelings that accompany the thought. If you don't have experience identifying your thoughts and emotions, it might be difficult at first. On the next page you will find some common Negative Body Thoughts and examples of possible emotional reactions.

Whether your Negative Body Thoughts are mild or extreme, you are sabotaging yourself and your life in subtle or not-so-subtle ways. This list is by no means exhaustive; we all have our particular brand of Negative Body Thoughts, and we all have unique feelings that result from them.

Thought	Feeling
I am so fat.	Embarrassment, shame, guilt
The cellulite on the back of my thighs is disgusting.	Horror, disgust, hopelessness
I wish I had her legs.	Jealousy, anger, self-pity
My butt is way too big.	Inadequacy, shame, disgust
If I gain weight, I will hate myself.	Fear, lack of control
She is thinner [or better, more attractive, etc.] than I am.	Inadequacy, inferiority
If I had her body, I would be happy.	Jealousy, frustration
I can't look in the mirror; I am too hideous.	Terror, fear, disgust
If only I lost those extra 10 pounds, then I would be [happy, successful, lovable, in a successful relationship, etc.].	Incapable, inadequacy, hopelessness
My age is really beginning to show.	Defeat, lack of control, resignation
With these wrinkles my face looks like a dried prune.	Inadequacy, frustration, resignation
I wish I had my pre-pregnancy body.	Dissatisfaction, defeat, hopelessness
I looked so much better when . . .	Sorrow, resignation, fatigue
I am so ugly!	Inadequacy, failure, embarrassment

Notice that I have also included thoughts about other people's bodies. In truth, there is no difference between the two. The way you look at yourself is the way you look at other people, and the way you look at other people is the way you look at yourself. If you are judgmental of yourself, you will be judgmental toward others. If you are critical toward others, you will be critical toward yourself. The beauty of this, however, is that when you learn to love yourself, you will love others, too.

Be sure to include Negative Food Thoughts as well, and just for fun (this IS fun, right?), add in any other negative thoughts about yourself and the feelings they evoke.

Identify Your Negative Thoughts—*continued*

Some possible examples are:

- I can't believe I ate that [chocolate, ice cream, doughnut, bread, etc.].
  I have no self-control; I am disgusting.
- As long as I control what I eat, I will be safe.
- I am so out-of-control; I shouldn't be allowed to be around food.
- I don't need to eat.
- I must constantly control what I eat.
- I get fat when I look at food.
- I just love food too much.
- I gain weight when I look at food.

Some other negative thoughts that might be lurking in your mind:

- I deserve to be treated this way by [partner, boss, coworker, etc.];
  I am so fat and disgusting.
- I shouldn't [ask for a raise, take a dance class, wear a swimsuit, go
  out with friends] because I am not thin enough, beautiful enough, etc.
- If I cannot control my body; I am a complete failure, regardless of
  other accomplishments in my life.
- I am selfish if I focus on my needs.
- I am just not that great.
- I am unworthy.
- I am not lovable.

If you have been struggling with this for years and your brain is programmed
with a seemingly endless slew of Negative Body Thoughts, get two notebooks! You may find that every other thought you have is a Negative Body
Thought. Not to worry; don't let your thoughts spin a story about how bad
you are or how hopeless you are. Simply identify and record every Negative
Body Thought that arises.

Discover Who Created Your Thoughts

As we have already discussed, your Negative Body Thoughts are not your own. They are recycled energy; quantum material circulating throughout the universe. Your particular thoughts are populating your mind because they have been fed to you by others since the day you were born. The same thing is true for the majority of everyone else's thoughts as well.

So get out the notebooks where you recorded your negative thoughts, beliefs, and behaviors. Ask yourself: Where did this thought come from? Where did this belief come from? Where did this behavior come from? Why is it showing up on the screen of your awareness? This may seem like a daunting task if you have hundreds of Negative Body Thoughts, but trust me: you will be astounded as you discover that none of these thoughts are your own.

It does not matter if the people you list are still living or have passed on; it does not matter if you have any continued contact with them or not. The only requirement is that their teachings, patterns, beliefs, and behaviors have impacted your thoughts, attitudes, and actions. As I said, your parents or parental surrogates will probably be atop your list. Your list might also include important teachers, friends, adversaries, siblings, your church pastor, youth group leader, or spiritual teacher. It might include your favorite magazine or TV show. It might even include your favorite character from a book or a movie.

Your Negative Body Thoughts are that wizard! When left unquestioned and unchallenged, they will direct your life in painful, confusing, and self-defeating directions. When you learn how to identify and investigate, however, you will discover that your thoughts can have no more power over you than the power you give them.

Your Family History

You probably traced many of your thoughts back to your family. This is simply because your parents or parental surrogates have the strongest ability to shape the content of your mind during your formative years. During your childhood, patterns, thoughts, and behaviors are established that stay with you throughout your life until you learn to challenge them.

Lily's Story

Take the example of Lily, who is fifty-nine years old, 5'4½" tall, and weighs between 105 and 110 pounds. Lily was the first girl after four boys in her family. She was a skinny child and her mother would insult her and try to force her to eat. Sadly, she would also beat her regularly, and food became the one area of Lily's life that she could control. Her mother consistently told her that she was too skinny and unattractive. When she was twelve years old, she began to fill out and develop a more womanly figure.

Despite the physical changes, however, Lily's insecurity about her appearance stayed with her throughout her life. Although she now feels okay about her body, she is constantly concerned with her face. As she has aged, the shape and elasticity of her face has changed. Every time she looks in the mirror, she berates herself for not being beautiful, just as her mother had so many years before.

When her boyfriend broke up with her, the first thought that came into her mind was that she was not attractive enough. This thought was an exact replica of what her mother had told her as a child. After fifty years, this *one thought* is still influencing her life and her behavior. It is still determining how she feels about herself.

Why Should I Bother Unloading My Feelings in a Letter?

It's probably difficult to write the letters in the next exercise, but it's also very important. After all, the Negative Body Thoughts you have identified have been *ruining your life*. They have been limiting your self-esteem, growth, and development. They have been robbing you of the joy, the energy, the abundance, and the vitality that you deserve. These thoughts have been controlling your life. It is natural to have very strong emotions toward these thoughts, and toward the people they came from.

Aren't I Being Mean, Though?

Understand that it is okay to have negative feelings toward people, even those people whom you love the most. These feelings do not mean that you love or care about them any less. In fact, we often feel the strongest negative emotions toward the people with whom we are the closest. Simply let yourself experience whatever emotions arise, knowing they do not, in any way, diminish your love or admiration for those people.

You are not condemning anyone through this process. Indeed, the people we are most affected by are usually the people whom we care for deeply. This is not about labeling your parents or anyone else "wrong." It is simply an opportunity to identify the thoughts that are keeping you trapped so that you can break free from self-defeating beliefs and behaviors.

Those of us who struggle with Negative Body Obsession, regardless of its severity, often blame ourselves and aim negative emotions toward ourselves. We get angry at *ourselves* for not having the right body, for not being beautiful, for not being perfect. This process helps you break free

Write Some Letters

Part 1: Now that you have identified the sources of your thoughts in the previous exercise, sit down and write each of them a letter (on paper or on a computer; either way is fine). In these letters, you want to tell them how they have impacted you, how they have influenced your thoughts and beliefs about your body. You are going to explain how you learned negative behaviors, beliefs, attitudes, and actions from them, and how it has affected your life. It is okay to feel angry, hurt, frustrated, disappointed—whatever comes up. Mention any negative emotions in the letter. The goal of this process is healing, but often we need to express our negative emotions as part of this process. It does not mean you love the person any less; it is simply a part of the healing. More on this later.

Once you have finished writing all the letters, put them in a safe place for use in a later exercise.

Part 2: You now have one more letter to write, a letter to Negative Body Obsession (or a letter to anorexia, bulimia, emotional or compulsive or binge eating, dieting, general body dissatisfaction—whatever resonates for you and your particular struggle).

So get out your paper and pen or your computer and acknowledge the role that NBO (or other condition) has played in your life. Did it keep you safe when your parents were fighting? Did it offer you the love that you never felt at home? Did it offer you solace when you felt unpopular? Did it provide you companionship when you felt painfully alone? Did it offer you hope when you were filled with despair? Understand why it developed and what role it has played in your life.

Now tell NBO how it has hurt you. How has it limited you? How has it controlled your life and prevented you from being healthy and happy? Make it clear that you are severing yourself from the relationship. Although you developed a relationship with NBO for a reason, it has served its purpose. Tell it that you no longer need it; you are ready to live life on your own. Make it clear in no uncertain terms that you are ending the relationship once and for all; it is no longer welcome in any aspect of your life. When you finish writing the letter, place it with the others for later use.

from this pattern by realizing that the problem is not, and never was, with you. The problem is with the self-destructive thoughts that have controlled you and your life.

Though everyone is guilty, remember that no one is to blame. The people who have influenced you most profoundly are certainly guilty— they have passed on these Negative Body Thoughts that are stopping you from living a life of peace, joy, and abundance. Yet they are not to blame. These negative beliefs, attitudes, and behaviors were passed to them from their parents and teachers. They did not know any better. They were simply passing on what they learned.

You now face the golden opportunity to stop the cycle. By becoming aware of these negative patterns, you can change them. You can learn a different way of being that you can then pass on to those around you.

Linda's Story

Consider the example of my coaching client, Linda. Linda is fifty-four years old and has struggled with anorexia for years. Although she is now fully functional, she has numerous health problems from her eating disorder. She remains underweight and continues to struggle with food and her body. Her struggle began during a brief period when she was overweight in high school. She recalls that her father used to tease her about her weight. She desperately wanted to please him and maintaining a thin body was one way she sought his approval.

Although he has now passed on, she continues to believe that she is only lovable if she is thin. She gets angry with herself when she does not meticulously control her food intake. Her father was unable to offer her unconditional love and acceptance. In an attempt to gain his love, Linda tortured her body and herself, believing that if she made herself thin enough, that if she made herself perfect, he would finally love her in the way she needed to be loved. She continues to condemn herself, being driven by the desire for love and approval from someone who could never and can never give it to her.

In order to break free, Linda must offer herself unconditional love and acceptance. She must acknowledge that her father did the best that he could, but it was not enough for her at that time. She did not receive the love that she desired and deserved. Now, however, she can offer herself the love and support that she craves. In doing this, she will be able to forgive her father and experience the unbounded and unconditional love that is her birthright.

Facing Eating Disorders

Realize that all the patterns, behaviors, and beliefs you have were created for a reason. This is especially true if you have struggled with an intense and often overwhelming condition such as an acute eating disorder or body hatred. Often, people develop these obsessions to help keep them safe from some threat in their life.

For many, an eating disorder has created safety where there was none; it created friendship when there was no one. It offered hope when there was despair; it offered tranquility in the face of anxiety. It gave direction when there was confusion and a voice when they felt mute.

There are very good reasons why you developed your obsessions and disorders. Unfortunately, these obsessions no longer serve you. Although an eating disorder, or any other negative pattern, can offer temporary relief, it will ultimately destroy you. It seduces you into believing you are in control, while in reality it is controlling you and will destroy you if given the chance. Fortunately, you can destroy it and reclaim your life.

Realize that as you begin to destroy Negative Body Obsession, you will need to address the emotions: the fear, the anger, the insecurity, and

Draw and Destroy

Now that you have identified Negative Body Thoughts, understand where they came from, and have unloaded your feelings about them, the time has come to destroy them so they no longer have any hold or influence on your life. For this exercise, you'll need a large piece of white posterboard, colored markers, a baseball bat, a pillow, and a brown paper bag.

Begin by drawing your view of your body and yourself on the white poster board with the markers. It does not have to be an exact drawing; rather, capture the way that you feel about your body. Draw the anger, the frustration, the disappointment, the anxiety, the guilt, the shame, the embarrassment. Then, with the remaining white space, write in your Negative Body Thoughts and the feelings that they result in. The entire piece of posterboard should be covered, first with your negative view of your body, then with your Negative Body Thoughts and feelings that accompany them.

When the drawing is complete, place it on a pillow. Start hitting the paper with the baseball bat. Use all your strength and energy to hit this piece of posterboard. It can be very helpful to use your voice, too. Yell, scream, and tell these thoughts that they are not your friends and they no longer have any place in your life. You can say something like:

> *"You are not my friend. You destroy my life. You strangle my creativity. You suck away my confidence. I no longer need you in my life. You may fight for your survival, but my light, my beauty, and my goodness will triumph. I no longer need you in my life. My light is so bright, my beauty so brilliant, that you cannot survive."*

As you continue to hit it, eventually the paper will begin to tear. Continue on like this until the piece of paper is nothing more than a pile of scraps. If you get tired of using the baseball bat, you can begin to tear the paper to pieces with your hands. When you have completely destroyed the posterboard, put the pile of shredded posterboard in a brown paper bag.

Draw and Destroy—*continued*

Add to the bag:

- The letters that you wrote to your parents, other people of influence, and NBO.
- Your notebooks filled with all of your Negative Body Thoughts.

Find a place where you can light a fire; be sure to be *very* safe and take all necessary precautions. Drop the brown bag into the flame. If you can't light a fire, throw the bag in a dumpster, or bury it—do whatever you want to destroy the bag and its contents. As you watch it burn or fall out of sight, repeat the following words:

> *"Negative Body Obsession, you are not my friend. You drain me of my vitality, my energy, and my enthusiasm. You seduce me into believing that I am not good enough. You trick me into believing that I am not beautiful enough, thin enough, strong enough, or important enough to live my life fully. You have stifled my creativity, you have strangled my divinity. You no longer have a place in my life. From this day forward, I will live in freedom, without your debilitating presence. From this moment on, I will live with peace, with joy, and with love, knowing I am eternally beautiful and worthy of all goodness and affection."*

This ritual marks the ending of your relationship with NBO and the beginning of your relationship with beauty, abundance, energy, and vitality. Congratulations!! Now that you have (mentally and literally) destroyed your Negative Body Thoughts and destructive beliefs, you are ready to connect with your true essence and discover the eternal beauty and vitality within you.

the pain that NBO or the eating disorder has helped you avoid. This can be scary and sometimes overwhelming. If you find that you need additional help with this process, please seek professional support. There is a list of resources in the appendix on page 213, including my signature five-step coaching program to help you through this process. You can also look in your hometown for a local psychotherapist who may be able to offer support.

Take a Bow

Those exercises were not easy, I know. But consider the weight you have lifted off your overburdened mind! You have come a long way in defeating NBO. The hardest part is over—you are more ready than ever to begin living the life you deserve. You have successfully pulled out the weeds, now you are ready to plant some flowers! Let's move on to creating some positive thoughts.

The Power of Positive Affirmations

Affirmations have incredible power and can help to transform your life. Here is a true story of how affirmations can create lasting transformation.

After learning about the power of affirmations, Sandra decided to try them with her daughter. Her daughter was in grade school at the time and had diagnosed learning disabilities. As a young child, she had already developed a core belief that she was stupid and couldn't learn. She was in special education classes, which reaffirmed her belief that she was academically deficient.

Sandra had her young daughter repeat the following affirmations every morning and evening. "I love myself"; "I am a smart person"; "I learn easily." Although her daughter was very resistant to what she considered a silly exercise, after six weeks of regular practice, amazing shifts

Positive Thoughts

Now that you have successfully identified and detached from your negative thoughts, let's fill your head with positive ones! You know this by now: your thoughts create your reality. If you think thoughts of joy, abundance, and love, you will begin to experience more joy, abundance, and love.

Your positive thoughts can be about anything in your life that you want. If you often found yourself thinking the negative thoughts below, for example, you now have positive substitutes:

Thought	Replace It With:
"I am so fat and ugly."	"I am inherently beautiful; I am honoring my body in everything I do. I am working with my body to make it as healthy and vibrant as possible."
"I am so lonely; food is my only companion."	"I am focusing on my true nature as always-expanding love. I am creating loving relationships and am learning how to feed myself appropriately in every area of my life."
"If only I lose weight; if only I remain thin, then everything will be okay."	"I am inherently lovable and worthwhile, regardless of what anyone thinks. I am completely safe and secure, being held in the arms of the entire universe."
"If I looked like her, then I would be happy."	"We are each a unique expression of the divine. I am beautiful; she is beautiful; he is beautiful; we are all beautiful."
"I will never have enough [love, food, money, abundance, peace, security, etc.]."	"Everything I desire is showing up in my life. I lack nothing. My intention will create what I desire."
"I am not good enough to do, be, or have anything I want."	"I am already perfect exactly as I am. I am worthy of having, being, or doing anything I desire."

Complete this exercise for every area of your life. These replacement thoughts can serve as affirmations for you to use to remind yourself of your inherent beauty and strength. Write them down on 3" × 5" index cards and carry them with you throughout the day. Look at them regularly. Remember, most of your thoughts are habitual. It took years to create and solidify your Negative Body Thoughts. It might take some time to create new patterns. The more you can practice and reinforce positive thoughts, the more automatic and habitual they will become.

Write Love Letters!

While developing positive thoughts, it can be helpful to engage in the same letter-writing process that you engaged in earlier. Write another round of letters to those same people who have had a profound influence on your life (your parents or parental figures, as well as any teachers or others who have profoundly affected your development).

The difference? This time, focus on how they have *positively* influenced your life. What thought patterns or behaviors have they given you that have served you well? How have they contributed to your success? How have their habits and insights helped you? How have these people contributed to your evolution and growth? If appropriate, you can even give these letters to them. Everyone loves to feel appreciated and acknowledged, and positively impacting another human being is the highest honor. If it is not appropriate or possible to give the letters to them, the writing process itself will have a dramatic impact on shifting your focus to the positive elements within yourself and your life.

started to occur. She started keeping up with her schoolwork. She developed and maintained a positive attitude. She began to excel academically. She started to focus on her core strengths and talents and use them to her advantage. Just by using these simple affirmations, the course of her life changed forever. She transformed from a failing student to an achieving student, while discovering her unique gifts and talents in the process.

Don't Take My Word for It . . .

Though I hope you believe me, I've got more proof that thinking positive thoughts is great for your overall well-being. Dr. Daniel Amen, a clinical neuroscientist and psychiatrist, has documented how our thoughts influence our physiology. By changing our thoughts, we can actually change our brains and thereby can transform our lives.

Here's how it works: Whenever you think a thought, your brain releases chemicals, then electrical transmissions travel throughout your brain, and you become aware of what you are thinking. When you have an angry, sad, mean, or negative thought, your brain releases negative chemicals that make your body feel bad. Your muscles become tense; your heart beats faster; your hands may start to sweat. Alternatively, when you think positive thoughts, your muscles relax, your heart rate slows, and you live in a calmer state. Amazingly, not only is your overall physiology affected, your actual brain is affected as well!

You can choose the thoughts you listen to.

One study of brain function at the National Institute of Mental Health investigated the brain activity of ten women. The study looked at a particular part of the brain (the deep limbic system) when women were thinking neutral thoughts, happy thoughts, and sad thoughts. This part of the brain is involved in setting emotional tone. When it is less active, the person is usually in a more positive, hopeful state of mind. When it is overactive, negativity becomes the norm.

Here's what happened:

- When the women thought neutral thoughts, nothing changed in their brains.
- When they thought happy thoughts, the women demonstrated less activity in the deep limbic system within their brains.
- With sad thoughts, the deep limbic system in the brain became highly active.

This study confirms that whenever you have a happy, hopeful, kind, loving, or friendly thought, your brain releases chemicals that actually help to calm your brain and help your body to feel good!

The bottom line—when you detach from negative thoughts and begin to focus on more positive ones, you can actually help to transform your brain. Furthermore, these positive thoughts will help to improve your health and overall well-being in every area of your life. Just *another* benefit to add to the list.

Points to Remember

- You are not your thoughts.
- Many of your thoughts were given to you by your parents or other people whom you were close to.
- You can decide which thoughts to listen to and which ones to ignore.
- Proactively identify and detach from the negative thoughts that are keeping you trapped.
- Replace with positive thoughts that will move you in the direction you want to go.

CHAPTER EIGHT

Step 3: Discover Who You Really Are

The thought of "discovering who you really are" might sound daunting, I know. But in order to rid yourself of Negative Body Obsession, you have to find your true identity. It's in there—but because you've suffered through years of Negative Body Thoughts, you will have to dive deep within yourself and connect with your essence that is beyond your thoughts. That's what we'll do in this chapter.

As you learn to dive past your thoughts into the reservoir that you truly are, you will discover your amazing majesty. As Deepak Chopra says in *The Seven Spiritual Laws of Success*, "We will remain unfulfilled unless we nurture the seeds of divinity inside us. In reality, we are divinity in disguise, and the gods and goddesses in embryo that are contained within us seek to be fully materialized. True success is therefore the experience of the miraculous. It is the unfolding of divinity within us. It is the perception of divinity wherever we go, in whatever we perceive—in the eyes of a child, in the beauty of a flower, in the flight of a bird. When we begin to experience our life as a miraculous expression of our divinity—not occasionally, but all the time—then we will know the true meaning of success." And no matter what you're struggling with—weight, hatred of a particular body part, frustration with aging—you probably want to experience success and happiness all the time, right?

What Does Your Ideal Life Look Like?

I want to begin this chapter by asking you a few questions. Take a moment to write down your responses before continuing.

- What would your life look like if you truly believed, without a shadow of a doubt, that you were beautiful?
- What would your life look like if you believed you had the best body in the world?
- What would your life look like if you believed you were unequivocally attractive enough, qualified enough, and deserving enough to be, do, and have anything that you desired?
- What would your life look like if you were not obsessed about your weight and being thin?

You Should *Have* Your Ideal Life!

If the exercise showed that your ideal life looks any different than it currently does, you are selling yourself short. You are settling for a life of mediocrity when you deserve a life of abundance. You are accepting a life of surviving instead of a life of thriving. You are accepting a vision of limitation instead of fulfilling your potential. You have traded your true identity for a false interpretation. In short, you are living a life based on delusion instead of a life based on reality. But, luckily, when you reclaim your identity, your true potential can shine.

This chapter will help you make an identity shift from small, uninspired, and weak to great, brilliant, magnificent, and beautiful. In order to do this, you must discover who you truly are and learn to connect with your "eternal essence."

The first step in this journey of reclaiming your true identity begins with understanding the different levels of your existence. For some of you, this information may be totally new and even a little surprising. Keep an open mind and imagine what you can accomplish with this knowledge.

Level 1: The Physical Domain

The first level of existence is the physical domain. This is the domain that you are probably most familiar with and where most people focus the majority of their attention. This is the domain that is perceived and experienced through the five senses of taste, touch, smell, hearing, and sight. It is dictated by cause and effect, action and reaction. It is inherently unstable and constantly changing. Everything in this domain is marked by a beginning, a middle, and an end; for example, there is birth, life, and death. Unfortunately, when we live exclusively in the physical or material world, we are bound to suffer and suffer greatly. We will seek permanence in a world of constant change; we will grasp for solidity in a world of ongoing fluctuation.

Beauty is everywhere, all the time. True beauty is eternal.

The Bad News

Those who struggle with Negative Body Obsession have an intimate experience of the pain that comes from exclusive identification with physical reality. Think of it: Your body is constantly changing. Second by second, minute by minute, hour by hour, your physical body is in a constant state of birth, life, and death; generation, sustenance, and destruction (think of cells growing, dividing, dying, etc.). When you try to maintain a constant body weight or control your body, you are orchestrating your own frustration because you are at odds with the very nature of the physical domain. You grasp for permanence, but there's none to be had.

In terms of your mind and thoughts, you attempt in vain to satisfy the needs of the ego. You fight for approval, for safety, for love, and for control by obsessing and attempting to control your physical body. This fight is doomed to failure, too. You can never create permanency out of the impermanent; you can never find solace in controlling your body; you can never find approval when you grasp for it. Your attempts to measure your success and well-being through your weight or your clothing size are inherently flawed.

The bottom line: You can never become truly beautiful when you seek perfection in the physical realm alone.

The Good News

What is truly breathtaking, however, is that you are entitled to the very beauty, success, glory, and greatness that you desire. It is only when you move into absolute and unconditional acceptance of your body and yourself, however, that you can ultimately find the glory and beauty within you. From the place of unconditional love and acceptance comes the unparalleled greatness of who you really are.

You are already perfect; you are already radiant, you are already truly beautiful. When you discover this, anything is possible.

Level 2: The Energetic Domain

The next level of reality is the energetic domain. This is the level of existence that is beyond our five senses but nevertheless scientifically validated. The energetic domain includes aspects of ourselves, such as our mind, with thoughts and emotions, as well as our ego, which gives the perception of "me" and "mine." We cannot see our mind, but we know that it exists. We cannot see our thoughts and emotions, but we experience them constantly. We cannot see our ego, but we experience it often, with its constant chatter.

Everything in the physical realm has an energetic foundation. Your body, like every physical object, is made up of atoms. These atoms, in turn, are made up of smaller molecules that are essentially vibrating energy containing information. So everything in the physical world, including your own body, is energy and information that you perceive to be a solid object. The reason we perceive solid objects instead of energy and information is because our senses function too slowly to register what is happening at the energetic level.

So everything we perceive to be solid is really not solid at all. Rather, it is constantly moving as it vibrates at this level. When scientists investigated this domain, they discovered that everything is constantly flickering on and off, constantly appearing and disappearing. Since energy is moving so quickly, our senses perceive it to be constant. It is like an old movie reel of still pictures that move so quickly they appear to be animated.

Level 3: The Spiritual Domain

Believe it or not, there is a level of existence that is even more subtle than the energetic level. This is the aspect of existence that is the ground for everything else—it is the field from which everything in the entire universe emanates (for that reason, it's often referred to as "the Source"). It cannot be perceived through the five senses, nor with the assistance of a microscope, but it can be experienced. This has been called the spiritual domain, the non-local domain, the virtual domain, the field of pure potential, and the field of all possibilities.

When we are disconnected from this Source, our lives are marked by anxiety, insecurity, obsessions, and emotional turbulence. When we are aware of and connected to this Source, our lives are characterized by peace, love, authenticity, energy, and vitality.

It can be quite difficult to conceptualize this spiritual or non-local domain because it is beyond time and space. So if you're having trouble grasping it, don't worry. There are no words that describe it, yet you can have a direct experience of it.

Attributes of the Source

Let me explain further by identifying attributes of this field, of this Source. As you strengthen your connection to your Source, your life begins to manifest more of your desires and more of your dreams are fulfilled. They might remind you of the attributes of the field of intention that we talked about on page 36. Just as with that field, you want to do your best to live the Source attributes in order to attract them to your life. The Source displays these qualities:

- Unconditional love
- Eternal beauty
- Constant creativity
- Gentle receptivity
- Unwavering kindness
- Constant expansion
- Boundless compassion
- Unlimited abundance
- Incredible joy
- Boundless energy
- Ecstatic bliss

Luckily, we are eternally connected to this field, for it is our Source and the Source of everything that ever was, is, or is to come. We can never truly be separate from it because it has breathed us into existence.

When you believe that you're separate from the Source (or you deny that the Source exists), however, you disconnect from it and lose the strength of its power in your life. You disconnect by favoring the ego, with its need for approval and admiration, and when you deny the brilliance, beauty, and glory that you are at this very moment. When you live with ego as your Source, you are doomed to anxiety, loneliness, depression, and frustration.

How the Ego Is Different

The ego is an illusory thought-construct that we have developed about who we are. Our ego is the thought patterns that tell us we are what we look like, what we have, or what other people think about us. The ego tells us that we are separate, isolated individuals with no connection to our Source. Living from your ego results in hosts of maladies and frustrations because you lose your connection to abundance, creativity, energy, and vitality.

Some of the attributes of the ego-based mindset are:

- Fear
- Isolation
- Insecurity
- Competition and needing to be better than someone else
- Greed
- Worry
- Hatred
- The constant need for external approval
- Inadequacy
- Weakness
- Force

This list probably has a few things in common with the Negative Body Thought/Feeling list you came up with on page 80, doesn't it? That's because Negative Body Obsession is a disease of the ego. By living with NBO, you are cutting yourself off from the Source and from its power and potential in your life.

That's right: every time you look in the mirror with disgust and disdain, every time you mourn the size of your belly or your thighs, you disconnect yourself from the Source of all beauty, power, energy, and grace.

You Can Always Go Home Again

Although the ego demands that you disconnect from the Source, the Source is still always there for you, no matter what. The Source provides creativity, energy, kindness, love, and expansion, and you have access to all of these attributes; they are an essential part of your makeup. So no matter how long you've lived with NBO (thanks to your ego), you can always return to the great resources the Source offers.

Whether you experience these attributes, however, is up to you. If you choose to dislike your body and yourself, you can remain in the small world of ego. If you choose to love your body and yourself, appreciating beauty in yourself and everyone around you, then you can live in a world full of mystery, wonder, abundance, and magnificence.

I'm going to take a wild guess that you'd rather live a life of magnificence. Here are some exercises to help you connect with your spiritual domain and your Source.

Learn to Meditate

Meditation is a powerful method for connecting with the Source. There are a host of psychological, physiological, and spiritual reasons why meditation is so effective—you may know friends and family members who meditate on a regular basis for any number of

Your true identity is one of boundless potential and unsurpassed beauty.

benefits. The psychological and physiological effects of meditation have been well documented in the scientific literature. The spiritual benefits have been experienced and reported by countless individuals throughout history and the present day.

The beauty of meditation is that it allows us direct access to the spiritual level of existence. When we limit our existence to the first level (physical) or the first two levels (physical and energetic) of reality, we cut ourselves off from the spiritual level, which houses the power and inspiration you need to better your life. Most people live in a state of awareness that only includes the physical world of objects and the energetic world of thoughts and feelings. With consistent practice of meditation, though, you can gain access into the subtle world of the Source.

Once you have access to this Source, you can dip into the energy and creative impulse of the universe. The more you connect with your Source through meditation, the closer you become to it. The attributes of the Source then begin to manifest themselves more and more in your everyday thoughts, emotions, and behaviors.

There are many different meditation techniques currently available. If you already have a meditation practice that you find helpful, continue using it. If, on the other hand, you don't have a meditation practice or want to change the one you currently use, here are some suggestions.

So-Hum Meditation

So-Hum meditation is an ancient, easy, and highly effective form of meditation. In this practice, the sounds "So" and "Hum" are used as a mantra to help you connect with the deeper layers of your existence. *Mantra* literally means an "instrument of the mind." The mantra is used as an instrument to help you connect with your Source.

By using a mantra, you can interrupt the incessant NBO story that is playing constantly and chronically in your psyche. By interrupting this storyline little-by-little, you can begin to access that part of you that is beyond story, beyond the workings of the ego.

To practice "So-Hum" meditation, follow these steps:

1. Find a quiet place and sit comfortably. Close your eyes and become aware of your breath.
2. When you inhale, silently repeat the word "So". When you exhale, silently repeat the word "Hum". Every time you inhale, silently repeat the word "So"; every time you exhale, silently repeat the word

"Hum". Whenever your mind wanders, simply bring your attention back to the mantra.

3. Practice this for ten, twenty, or thirty minutes in the morning and the evening to help connect with your deeper dimension.

Primordial Sound Meditation

Primordial Sound meditation was developed by well-known authors, physicians, and spiritual teachers Deepak Chopra and David Simon. It is a mantra-based technique similar to So-Hum, the only difference being that you receive an individualized mantra based on your birth date, location, and time. There are Primordial Sound meditation instructors around the world. Please visit the resource section on page 213 to find an instructor in your area.

Don't Be Afraid to Ask for Help

Don't worry! If meditation doesn't immediately come naturally to you, join the club. When you are first learning meditation, it can be very difficult. If you have not been practicing sitting still, don't be surprised if you feel like you want to crawl out of your skin! This is natural. Remember, it is all about habits. It will take time to become comfortable with sitting still. Be patient and easy with yourself. It will become easier, but it will take some time. It can be helpful to have a teacher guide you and answer any questions or challenges that may come up. Be sure to check the resources in the appendix, or check online for centers and instructors in your local area.

Letting go of judgment is your pathway to *freedom*.

If You're Feeling Overwhelmed . . .

If you are in the midst of an intense struggle with Negative Body Obsession right now and your emotions are overwhelming and overpowering, please turn to the section on befriending your body and begin with the first exercise on page 139, the practice of mindfulness meditation.

You do not become beautiful by *trying* to be beautiful, but by *finding* the beauty that is *already within you*, and allowing that beauty to *emerge*.

If you are in the midst of intense emotional and physical turmoil, it is most helpful to first create a space or container to experience your emotions and learn that you can experience them without needing to flee. After you become familiar with the mindfulness practice, you can return to this section and practice So-Hum meditation or contact a Primordial Sound meditation instructor near you.

Using Affirmations

Throughout this chapter, you will see Key Affirmations in bold. As already discussed, affirmations can help you to create whatever you desire in your life. Remember, what we think about helps to create our reality. Repeating these affirmations will help you create the peace, love, and beauty that you desire. These affirmations can be used in the following ways:

1. Write the affirmations on index cards and read through them before you go into your meditation. Read the card, repeat the affirmation silently or out loud, and then go into your meditation using the So-Hum technique or another technique that you have learned. You don't want to repeat the affirmation during your meditation; just repeat it beforehand. By repeating the affirmation before meditation, you harness the creative power of the universe that will help you manifest the affirmation in your life.
2. Read through the affirmations when you wake up, during lunchtime, and before you go to bed. Studies have shown that your subconscious

mind is most easily influenced right after you wake up and right before you go to sleep. Reading the affirmations during these times will help reprogram your mind and your subsequent reality more rapidly.

3. Repeat the affirmations any time throughout the day. If you find yourself challenged by Negative Body Thoughts, you can repeat the affirmations to help create a new mental habit. If you find yourself feeling great about your body and your life, repeat the affirmations to help solidify your newfound sense of well-being. There is no need to be compulsive about it; just repeat these affirmations as you go through your day, whenever you think of it. Over time it will become a habit, and they will exert a positive influence on your life without your even having to think about it.

The Nature of Beauty

As we discussed in the chapter "How Did This Happen?" the perception of beauty in the physical domain is subject to time, place, and a particular society's outlook. Contrary to popular belief, beauty—in any time or place—is not something that is available only to the genetically gifted. Because true beauty emanates from the spiritual domain, it is available to all of us, all the time, in

Your relationship with the world is a *mirror* of your relationship with yourself.

infinite supply. Beauty is something that we can choose to create in our lives, second by second, minute by minute, hour by hour, by connecting with this spiritual domain.

There is no such thing as less beautiful or more beautiful when you are connected to the Source of all beauty. As you become aware of beauty, you create more beauty and receive more beauty. Eventually beauty will

Find Beauty in Everyone and Everything Around You

Key Affirmation: "There is beauty in everything; there is beauty everywhere; beauty is eternal."

The following exercises and discussions are designed to help you connect with the Source so you can enjoy its benefits. In this exercise, the goal is to shift your awareness from a mindset that is judgmental and sees some people or things as beautiful and others as ugly to one that sees the beauty in everyone and everything. Here are a few ways you can begin to shift your habitual thinking:

When you find yourself having a judgmental thought, such as "Oh, she's fat" or "I look better than she does" or "She definitely should not be wearing that bathing suit," practice dropping the judgment. Instead, repeat this phrase: "There is beauty in everything; there is beauty everywhere; beauty is eternal." Extend the same practice to yourself. Whenever you look in the mirror and find yourself critiquing the cellulite on the back of your thighs, practice seeing beauty. There is beauty everywhere and in everything—it is simply up to you to find it.

follow you everywhere (since beauty exists in the spiritual domain, there is nowhere that beauty is not!).

The exercise on the following page will help you to both create and be receptive to beauty in all of its different manifestations.

Find Beauty in Yourself

Key Affirmation: "I am beautiful; I am beauty."
Even if you are able to cultivate appreciation for other people and the world around you, you probably still look at yourself with critical eyes. NBO's influence allows you to appreciate the beauty in other people's bodies, but forces you to continue to look at yours with disgust and contempt. For example:

- You accept that other people's bodies change and develop, yet you demand that yours remain the same.
- You tell people not to worry if they eat a doughnut now and then, but demand rigid control for your own diet.
- You allow others to be human but refuse to extend that same loving compassion toward yourself.

When you look at it this way, isn't it backward, unfair, and sad? You should not live this way! The me-them construct you're experiencing is completely fabricated by your ego. When you are connected to the Source, you realize that there is no me and them; there is no me and you. You can see the same amount of beauty outside yourself that you see inside yourself.

Eckhart Tolle writes, "You do not become good by trying to be good, but by finding the goodness that is already within you, and allowing that goodness to emerge." The same can be said of beauty—you do not become beautiful by trying to be beautiful, but by finding the beauty that is already within you, and allowing that beauty to emerge. Begin

Create a Collage

Creating a collage is a potent tool for transforming your vision, concept, and experience of beauty. Gather pictures of people's faces and bodies, places, artwork—anything that evokes a sense of beauty to you. Now gather pictures of people, places, artwork, etc., that you *don't* consider beautiful, even those that you consider ugly. Make these into a collage, either as two separate collages or all together into one.

Place your work somewhere you will see it on a regular basis. Practice finding the beauty in both sets of pictures. Initially, it will be easy to locate beauty in the pictures you already consider beautiful, but practice cultivating this same sense of beauty in that which you initially deemed ugly. Over time, you will find that your segregation of beauty/ugliness was a mental construct—you will identify beauty in both categories of art.

Please note: If you are in the grips of Negative Body Obsession or an eating disorder, realize that it will attempt to delude you at every turn. You probably have developed a delusion that says ultra-thin is beautiful. Even if you are successful in cultivating a sense of beauty and appreciation for all body types, NBO might still convince you that you are only beautiful if you are rail thin. It might also justify self-starvation: since everything is beautiful, why not starve yourself and be super-thin because that is your beauty preference?

As usual, the solution to this lies in first becoming aware and being completely honest with yourself about what NBO is saying. Then begin to ask yourself: Is my vision of beauty healthy? Does it promote energy and vitality? Does this body look healthy? Is my behavior around food healthy? Am I at peace?

today by locating the beauty within you and allow it to radiate out into the world.

The following exercise will help you learn to look at yourself with beauty and appreciation.

Try Visualization

How would you feel about yourself if you truly believed you were beautiful?

As we discussed in Step 2, science has shown us that visualization is an extremely powerful tool in changing any part of your life, from physical and emotional health to relationships to financial well-being. Your brain uses exactly the same processes whether you are visualizing something or actually engaging in the activity/living in that state. When you visualize yourself as beautiful, radiant, sexy, energetic, and comfortable, you begin to create that for yourself. Imagine the appreciation you feel for your body, as well as the vitality and energy you experience. By doing this, you begin the process of creating this experience in your life.

Try incorporating visualization after you finish your daily meditation exercises. Spend a few minutes visualizing yourself as beautiful, radiant, and energetic. How do you feel in your body and about your body? What would you do with your body if you felt truly beautiful? What would you do with your life? Visualize how you would feel and what your life would look like if you truly felt beautiful.

Forgive

A hallmark of Negative Body Obsession is self-hatred, or its milder yet still destructive cousin, self-dissatisfaction. Many of my clients attack themselves intensely and vigilantly whenever they eat too much or fail

Talking to Yourself in the Mirror

This is a valuable exercise that I have adapted from Jack Canfield's book *The Success Principles*. Every evening before you go to bed, take off your clothes and stand in front of a full-length mirror. Look at your body and tell it that you love it. Offer yourself unconditional love and acceptance by repeating: "I am beautiful; I am beauty."

I know this can seem like a daunting prospect if you have a habit of hating, or at the very least disliking, your body. For many, this exercise might sound unbearable. "What, are you crazy?!! Look at myself in a mirror naked?! Never!" If it seems impossible to complete this exercise, that is okay. Be gentle with yourself. There was a time when I could not stand the idea of looking at myself in the mirror—I was too afraid. But over time, as I began to heal, I learned to look at myself with love, affection, and appreciation. My advice is to be easy with yourself. You can practice looking at yourself in the mirror with your clothes on, appreciating your body. As you heal, you will gradually be able to complete this exercise in its entirety.

As you become more comfortable with this exercise, find specific areas of your body that you like and start praising them individually. Every night before bed, practice this exercise, offering your body gratitude and appreciation. It is also helpful to offer yourself gratitude and appreciation for other accomplishments and achievements of the day. Congratulate yourself for giving your friend a hug or a compliment; offer yourself appreciation when you held the door open for someone. Offer yourself love for no reason at all, simply because you are a beautiful, unique, worthy, worthwhile individual.

We all have a deep longing to be loved, acknowledged, and appreciated. The surest way to get the love you need is to begin to offer it to yourself on a regular basis. Be sure to practice this every night, even if it feels awkward at first. Many of us have never received this unconditional love. Repetition is essential as you reprogram your relationship with yourself.

Spend Time in Nature

Key Affirmation: "As nature is, so am I."

Do you look at a flower and marvel at its intricate beauty? Do you stand in front of the ocean and find yourself swept away by its vast glory? Do you stand among trees and feel nurtured by their majesty? Do you gaze at the stars and get lost in the empty space? Rarely do we give ourselves the time to marvel at the greatness that surrounds us. Learning to appreciate what's around you, however, is an important part of learning to appreciate what is inside of you.

Why? Because whatever you see outside of you is within you, too. That's right: scientifically speaking, you are made up of the same exact atoms, molecules, and particles that make up the trees, the stars, and the ocean. On an atomic and subatomic level, you and nature are exactly the same; you are just arranged differently. You are stardust incarnate, the vastness of the ocean personified, the strength of a tree embodied. You are the very things that you consider beautiful, and so you must be beautiful yourself.

Spend time in nature contemplating its beauty and glory. Repeat this affirmation to yourself: "As nature is, so am I." Practice experiencing this beauty outside of yourself; then bring your attention inward and practice seeing beauty within you. Alternate back and forth in this way until you can see the same beauty within yourself that you can see outside of yourself.

to live up to their predetermined standards. Feeling too full or gaining weight can spark hatred, disgust, shame, embarrassment, and an overwhelming sense of failure. Sufferers berate themselves, engaging in mental self-mutilation and verbal abuse. Whenever—and I mean *whenever*—we attack and condemn ourselves, we are attacking the Source and diminishing our connection to it. Another effective way to connect to the Source is through the practice of forgiveness.

Forgive Yourself

Key affirmation: I forgive; I am forgiving; I am forgiven.

For those struggling with NBO, the place to begin forgiveness is often within your own self, body, mind, and spirit. Have you not taken the best care of your physical body? Forgive yourself. Have you overindulged? Have you underindulged? Have you exercised too much or not enough? Forgive yourself. Have you judged yourself harshly? Have you judged others harshly? Forgive yourself. Have you hurt yourself mentally, emotionally, or physically? Forgive yourself.

You are worthy of absolute, unwavering, and immediate forgiveness. When you forgive yourself you rekindle your connection to the Source; you align your spirit with the creative energy of the universe. When you forgive yourself you clear a pathway for true beauty to shine through.

Forgive Others

As we extend forgiveness to ourselves, we must extend that forgiveness to others. Look back at the letters you wrote in the exercise "Write Some Letters" on page 86; think back to the people who have influenced your thoughts and your development of NBO. These people did the best they could from their state of awareness. Although they may be guilty, they are not to be blamed. If you are unable to forgive someone, you are the one who will suffer. When you are unable to forgive, you create an energetic block between you and the Source. You limit the flow of energy between you and the universe.

On the other hand, when you extend forgiveness to yourself and everyone in your life you align yourself with your Source. You connect with the creative impulse of the universe that will aid you in the fulfillment of your desires.

This book is about finding your freedom, and the ability to forgive is an essential component in this quest for freedom. Try repeating this mantra: "I forgive; I am forgiving; I am forgiven" before your daily meditation. You can use the exercises on the next page to help you in the process.

Cultivate Gratitude

Cultivating gratitude for yourself and others is another way to connect to the Source. In her book, *Happy for No Reason*, Marci Shimoff cites some of the cutting-edge research on the other benefits of gratitude. People who describe themselves as feeling grateful tend to:

- Have more vitality and optimism
- Suffer less stress
- Experience fewer episodes of clinical depression than the population as whole

Gratitude is more than simply a nice idea—it is an essential component in helping you transform your life for the better. NBO is characterized by a lack of gratitude toward your body and yourself. The vast majority of us have long-ingrained habits of critiquing our bodies and ourselves, never believing we are quite beautiful enough or good enough. Replace the habit of self-condemnation with gratitude. Transform your critical eye into an eye that recognizes and is grateful for the displays of beauty inside and outside of yourself.

Make gratitude a habit. Just as you have developed a habit of criticizing your body, you can develop a habit of being grateful for it. I know this can be difficult at first if you have suffered from physical illness or

Revisit Your Letters

Take yourself back to when you wrote the letters to the people who influenced your thoughts and the development of Negative Body Obsession (see page 86). Recall everything they did that hurt and angered you. Now focus on *why* they did these things. Realize that any pain they have inflicted on you is pain they have within themselves, whether they are conscious of this or not. The pain they have inflicted on you has also brought more pain into their lives. As you focus on the pain and hurt they have undergone, you will find your heart begin to soften. Around the anger and the pain, the seeds of compassion will be planted.

Now take out a pen and paper and begin to write letters of forgiveness. Write letters to every person who has hurt you and caused you pain, forgiving him or her. Tell them that you understand why they did what they did. You don't need to condone their actions; indeed, people often do horrific and dreadful acts. Yet you can feel the pain that prompted these actions and the pain that resulted from these actions. As you continue to write, it will get easier and the suffering will begin to transform into compassion.

If you are highly visual, you can even make a forgiveness drawing. Draw what it feels like when you extend forgiveness and compassion to those who have hurt you. You can draw their pain and realize that through your compassion and empathy, you are in some way beginning to ease pain and suffering.

have a lifelong habit of condemning and being dissatisfied with your body. Please remember, however, that what you put your attention on grows. Gratitude helps you align with the Source and allows happiness to flow into your life. The hands-on exercises on the following page will help you incorporate gratitude into your day.

Let Go of Judgment

Key Affirmation: There is no freedom in judgment.
When we judge ourselves and other people, we suffer—period. You are meant to be free to experience the joy, creativity, and possibility that freedom brings. When you judge yourself and other people, you deny yourself this freedom. Yet, body judgment is the norm for many people in our culture. When people with NBO see themselves and other people, their first reaction is to condemn, critique, analyze, and opine about their bodies. In Step 2 you became intimately familiar with the particular chronic thoughts and judgments that reside in your psyche. A judgmental dialogue often sounds something like this:

> *Hmmm, she really needs to lose a little weight. She would look so much better if she would exercise more often. Wow—I look so much better than her—I am glad I don't have her butt. Oh, but her thighs—I wish I had her thighs! If only I had her thighs . . . She is so much more attractive than I am—that means she is more successful. No wonder she has a boyfriend and a new car; it's because of those legs! But I hope I never look like her—I don't know how I would live if I had her looks—at least my breasts are bigger than hers . . . .*

On and on drones this ridiculous voice of judgment and comparison. You might have thoughts about someone else's body, or bank account, or relationship, or anything else that you use to judge yourself relative to someone else. And it's ubiquitous in modern culture—it only takes

Write It Down

Every night before going to bed, write down a list of what you are grateful for that day. Begin with what you are grateful for about your body. How has your body served you today? The chronic tendency is to focus on what we don't like and what it *hasn't* done; let these thoughts pass. Did your body carry you where you needed to go? Did it fight away potential infections and illness? Did it allow you to exercise or dance or enjoy some aspect of being in the world? Our bodies are the vessels that allow us to experience and interact with the world. Without them, we would have no container for interacting with our environment. Write down what you are grateful for, and what you have to be grateful for will grow.

Change Your Thoughts to Grateful Ones

Key Affirmation: I am thankful. I am grateful for my body and for the beautiful abundance in my life.

Gratitude extended to our own selves and bodies unleashes a powerful transformative energy that will help us heal and grow into the people we want to become. Make gratitude an ever-present thought in your mind. Every time you find yourself critiquing and condemning your body, disengage from the Negative Body Thought using the techniques outlined in Step 2. Then consciously replace the Negative Body Thought with an affirmation of gratitude, such as the one above. As you transform your habits from destructive patterns of self-critique into habits of gratitude, you will witness the transformation of your life on every level.

a glance at the cover of *People* magazine or the latest gossip columns to see commentary on who has gained or lost weight, and how bad or good they now look.

You probably know what I'm going to say: This way of thinking leads only to suffering. If you listen to this judgmental voice, it will create suffering for yourself and the world around you, plain and simple. Fortunately, you do not need to listen to this voice. You can detach from these thoughts and change your inner dialogue as we talked about in Step 2. Practice repeating the affirmation above; "There is no freedom in judgment."

As you practice the exercises in this book and begin a regular practice of meditation, you will become increasingly aware of your thoughts. Notice when you are caught in judgment, either toward yourself or someone else. Don't condemn yourself when you notice the judgments—this will simply add another layer of ego-based thinking to the mix. Instead, identify the thoughts; then detach from the judgment and focus instead on finding the beauty. This will help to align you with the Source, creating greater peace, joy, and abundance in your life and the world at large.

Banish Fear

Key Affirmation: I am safe; I am secure; I am protected.
Negative Body Obsession, and the ego more generally, feeds on fear. Fear is the currency that keeps NBO alive and in business. In fact, NBO most likely developed in an attempt to keep you safe from some type of danger in the past. Once in place, NBO creates *more* fear and perpetuates the fear-based myth of "not good enough." It creates a cyclical prison: you feel afraid and turn to food and NBO to help create a sense of safety.

You listen to the lies perpetuated by NBO claiming that you are not thin enough, young enough, strong enough, or beautiful enough to live your life fully. These lies then create greater fear. Your world gets smaller as you attempt either to control food and your body, or else lose all control.

You may become afraid that:

- You will gain weight
- You will never lose the weight you have gained
- You will never be able to control your eating
- The slightest misstep will result in total failure

These fears follow you wherever you go. What a nightmare!

The reality is that these fears are based on lies and delusion. NBO is a smoke-and-mirrors phenomenon. Whenever you offer yourself conditional love and acceptance, you are living in the world of illusion. Statements such as:

- "I am only beautiful if I am thin"
- "I will only be beautiful when I am thin"
- "I am only happy if and when I am thin"
- "I deserve to suffer for being overweight"
- "I am ugly because I am overweight"
- "I am a failure if I cannot control what I eat"

create an inherently miserable state of mind.

These beliefs create overwhelming fear because your sense of self-worth is conditional—it requires a specific outcome to occur. You know deep down that your sense of well-being is balancing on a precipice and might plummet at any time. This ego-based thinking creates fear, anxiety, and insecurity, leading you to often make unhealthy choices.

These overwhelming and debilitating fears are caused by delusions, but they are nonetheless very intense. The fear can and probably does feel very real. To end the cycle, first become aware of the fear, experience the feeling, and then work to change the story that is generating that fear. Remember, you can detach yourself from your feelings of fear (see Step 2). You could start by adding the affirmation above to the list to read before your daily meditation.

Shift Your Identity

Our lives are stories that we live out every day. We have beliefs about who we are, what we should do, what we are entitled to, and what we are worth that inform and create our existence. These stories are usually based on our ego and are thus limited.

Begin by identifying the stories and self-concepts that you are living out in your life right now. Have you staked your identity claim in some of the finite, limited, and conditional terms, such as "I will only be happy when/if am thin," "I am worthy or unworthy of love because of my body weight and physical appearance," "I am ugly," "I will never find love," "I do what other people recommend," "I am unlucky," "Bad things always happen to me," "I don't deserve to be happy," or "Life is unfair"? Sometimes you may barely notice these running thoughts since you are so used to hearing them. That's why just being aware of them is a big step.

Once you have identified some of your story lines, try this visualization:

- Sit quietly with your eyes closed. Think of one of the ego-based stories that you have identified. Tell yourself the story and experience the physical changes that the story creates. If it is a story based on fear, it will most likely result in your body feeling contraction, anxiety, and tightness.
- Now change the story; write yourself a new narrative. With your eyes still closed, picture yourself as radiant, powerful, and beautiful. Picture yourself as permanently connected to a never-ending Source of strength, beauty, and grace. You are forever radiant and beautiful, strong and supple, because you are forever connected to the Source that provides all of these things. Picture yourself as never failing in any of your endeavors. Although there may be bumps along the road, you will succeed because you have a permanent connection to the Source.

Shift Your Identity—*continued*

- As you visualize this truth, notice how it makes you feel. You should begin to feel expansive, powerful, and peaceful. The fear should slowly begin to subside and melt away. Use this visualization whenever you notice yourself gripped by fear.

You may find that this visualization is powerful enough to really help you disconnect from your ego-based story. This may produce a certain amount of fear. But don't give up. Simply close your eyes, take a few long, slow, deep breaths, and visualize your connection to the Source.

Then, as you go through your days, become increasingly aware of when you feel afraid. In these moments of fear, offer yourself unconditional love and support, affirming that you will always protect and care for yourself. Be gentle, yet persistent, and you will slowly transform the gripping fear into peace and serenity. The exercise starting on the previous page will help you with this process.

Remember How Amazing You Are

I want to conclude this chapter with the following poem and affirmation. Carry the poem with you and plant the affirmation in your heart. May you always experience the wisdom, beauty, and glory that you are.

The poem is from the Penguin publication *The Gift, Poems by Hafiz*, copyright © 1999 Daniel Ladinsky, and used with his permission.

Here's the affirmation: "I am an infinite field of boundless potential and unsurpassed beauty; may I always recognize my own greatness."

We Have Not Come Here to Take Prisoners

We have not come here to take prisoners,
But to surrender ever more deeply
To freedom and joy.

We have not come into this exquisite world
To hold ourselves hostage from love.

Run my dear,
From anything
That may not strengthen
Your precious budding wings.

Run like hell my dear,
From anyone likely
To put a sharp knife
Into the sacred, tender vision
Of your beautiful heart.

We have a duty to befriend
Those aspects of obedience
That stand outside of our house
And shout to our reason
"O please, O please,
Come out and play."

For we have not come here to take prisoners
Or to confine our wondrous spirits,

But to experience ever and ever more deeply
Our divine courage, freedom, and
Light!

—Hafiz

Points to Remember

- There are three different levels of existence: the physical, the energetic, and the spiritual.
- The spiritual domain is where you want to go to create a life of beauty, abundance, and success. It is where you can fulfill your desires.
- Ego-based thought patterns interfere with our connection to the Source.
- Negative Body Obsession is a disease of the ego. When we listen to NBO, we distance ourselves from the field of all possibilities.
- Review and practice these ideas and exercises for connecting with your Source:

  - Meditate.
  - Find beauty in everyone and everything.
  - Spend time in nature.
  - Practice forgiveness.
  - Cultivate gratitude.
  - Let go of judgment.
  - Banish fear.
  - Shift your identity.

CHAPTER NINE

Step 4:
Befriend Your Body

So far in this program, you have taken charge of your mind and connected with the spiritual domain, where you can access an endless supply of beauty and love. Now, you are going to fall in love with your body.

I realize that sounded very simple—I know it probably won't happen at the drop of a hat. After all, NBO has been telling you for years to hate your body. If you have been trapped in a routine of hating your body, you are in for an amazing surprise. Your body is truly awe-inspiring, as you'll see. Unfortunately, you have likely been ignoring and berating your body for so long, it's difficult to accept how stunning it is. Consider these quotes from Michelangelo:

- "A beautiful thing never gives so much pain as does failing to hear and see it."
- "What spirit is so empty and blind, that it cannot recognize the fact that the foot is more noble than the shoe, and skin more beautiful than the garment with which it is clothed?"

Have you been failing to see the beauty of your own body? Has your spirit been so depleted that it does not appreciate every aspect of your body? Have you been letting your idea of how you should look eclipse the beauty of who you are? If you answered yes to any of those questions, read on to find a renewed sense of appreciation for your physical body.

What Your Body Is Made Of

The first step in befriending your body is to understand that your body is merely an expression of an underlying energy field. As we discussed in the previous chapter, everything physical (such as your body) is made up of energy, and this energy emanates from an underlying quantum field. Your body appears to be a solid object because this is how your senses interpret the moving energy and information.

Your body is made up of three dimensions, much like the three levels of existence:

1. **A physical body:** This is the body that you are most familiar with—the one you can see and feel.
2. **An energetic body:** This is a more accurate depiction of your body, a field of energy, transformation, and intelligence.
3. **A causal (not *casual*) body:** This is the deepest level of your body, where your individual body merges with the underlying energy field.

The physical body is the most obvious and the one that has most likely given you the greatest challenge. The majority of this chapter is devoted to your physical body.

Here's a fun fact for you: Our bodies are 99.9 percent empty space. But, wait . . . we've got cells, organs, bones, and all sorts of other goodies in there. So how are we 99.9 percent empty space? According to physicists, your body is made up of atoms, which are particles moving at lightening speeds around huge empty spaces. These huge empty spaces come from the underlying energy field that we have been discussing, which is the reservoir of healing. Remember the field of intention, or this mysterious realm of your spirit? This empty space is the scientific explanation for the underlying energy field that we emanate from and of which we are a part. If you're aware of how that field literally lives in you, you are more able to access it.

Your Amazing Body

Our bodies are in a constant, dynamic, changing state. Just look at some of these mind-boggling statistics, found in Deepak Chopra's *Magical Body, Magical Mind*:

- Your body replaces 98 percent of its atoms in less than one year.
- You get a new liver every six weeks.
- You create a new skeleton every three months.
- You get a new stomach lining every five days.
- A whole new skin is generated every month.
- The cells in your brain weren't there last year; even your DNA as raw material did not exist six weeks ago.

As you can imagine, your body uses a substantial amount of energy to continue this process of constant rejuvenation. In fact, the body's greatest caloric need by far is simply the act of constant functioning on the cellular level. Your cells are very busy, keeping you healthy, powerful, and strong on a daily basis.

Where do our cells get the material to recreate us? Every time we breathe, we take in 10 to the power of 22 atoms from the universe that end up as our heart, kidneys, bones, and numerous other organs and tissues. Every time we exhale, we breathe out pieces of tissues and organs and recirculate them into the universe. We are constantly exchanging bits of our bodies with the bodies of everyone else on the planet. It's the ultimate form of recycling!

Cells

The cells within your body are conscious, living entities. Each cell is an intelligent being that can survive on its own, as scientists have demonstrated by removing individual cells from the body and growing them separately. Our bodies contain trillions of cells, and every function that exists in our entire body exists in each individual cell. Cell biologist Bruce Lipton explains that each eukaryote (which is any cell with a nucleus) possesses the equivalent of a nervous system, a digestive system, a respiratory system, an excretory system, an endocrine system, muscular and skeletal systems, a circulatory system, skin, a reproductive system, and even an immune system!

Cells and Thoughts

Every time you think, you influence your body's cellular activity. When you have a thought, feeling, or emotion, your nervous system generates a set of chemicals known as neuropeptides, which allow brain cells (and also other kinds of cells) to speak to one another. Each cell has receptors on its surface that recognize these chemicals. Brain and immune cells in particular are known for having these receptors.

What this means is that you cannot have an idea, thought, emotion, or desire without your immune cells knowing about it. Your immune cells are literally listening and reacting to your internal dialogue. Your entire body is constantly thinking, processing, adapting, and changing every second of every day, even while you are asleep.

Sufferers of Negative Body Obsession are notorious for expressing hatred toward their bodies, saying things like, "I am so fat! I hate my thighs, my arms, my butt, my stomach!" There is no question that such negative thoughts and emotions can profoundly influence our minds and bodies in a myriad of ways, many of which we are only now discovering. Fortunately, positive thoughts and emotions also have a profound effect, and as

Your body is in a constant state of *dynamic renewal*.

we learn to treat ourselves and our bodies with love and gratitude we can begin to transform ourselves and the world around us.

For an amazing pictorial representation of how your thoughts can affect your body, check out the work of Masaru Emoto at *www.masaru-emoto.net*. Emoto, a writer and researcher who lives and works in Japan, decided to photograph the crystals that form when water freezes. The unexpected results astounded him and suggest the power of our words to affect our health and well-being. Although Emoto's experimentation has been challenged for failing to adhere to the scientific method, including double-blind controls, his work can at the very least be understood as a photographic rendering of what has already been confirmed in numerous scientific studies.

Emoto found that crystal formation seems to reflect the words, music, or actions that water is exposed to as it freezes. Emoto and his colleagues wrote different words on paper, and then taped them onto bottles of water. They then froze the water and observed the crystals that formed. When water was exposed to the words "thank you," a beautiful hexagonal shape appeared. Conversely, when the water was exposed to the words "you fool," no crystals formed and the frozen water looked like a misshapen lump of ice.

Emoto's photographs hold possible implications for ourselves, our bodies, and our health. In the womb, fetuses are 99 percent water; infants are 90 percent water; and in adulthood our body is composed of 70 percent water. We are mostly water, and it is likely that we can and do influence this water, and therefore our bodies, in either positive or negative ways.

Clearly, our thoughts and our feelings have a direct influence on the world around us. The words we use and the emotional energy we radiate influence water and potentially everything around us. Given the dynamic nature of our bodies, and the fact that our bodies are predominantly water, these findings have profound implications for sufferers of Negative Body Obsession, and anyone else who doesn't feel absolute love for who they are.

Cells and Their Environment

While your body is listening and responding to your thoughts, emotions, and behaviors, it is also synchronizing itself with rhythms in the environment. Your body is constantly calibrating itself to daily cycles, lunar cycles, and seasonal cycles. Furthermore, all of your body processes are infinitely correlated, conducting an astounding number of processes at the same time. Your body can think thoughts, play an instrument, kill germs, make a baby, digest food, and watch the news all at the same time, while also coordinating with the environment outside.

This environmental calibration and synchronization also occurs on the cellular level. Cells have intent and purpose; they seek out environments that support their survival, while avoiding hostile environments that threaten their well-being. Just like our human bodies, our individual cells instantly analyze their environment and act to ensure their survival.

A look at individual cells confirms the ancient spiritual teaching that "as is the microcosm, so is the macrocosm"; as is the body, so is the universe and vice versa. What we see outside is a reflection of what is on the inside.

Your Body Is Also a Drugstore

If you aren't yet amazed at the wonders of the physical body, consider this: your body is also a self-prescribing pharmacy:

- When you feel tranquil, your body actually makes the natural equivalent of Valium.
- When you feel anxious, your body produces hormones such as adrenaline and cortisol.
- When you feel exhilaration, your body produces potent anticarcinogenic substances known as interferons and interleukins.

Our bodies produce an entire range of drugs, from antibiotics to tranquilizers, and our bodies make the exact amount at precisely the right time for the exact necessary use. Your body is in a constant state of dynamic exchange and calibration with your internal world of thoughts and emotions and your external world of the environment.

Your Body's Ability to Heal

You've no doubt seen everyday examples of your body healing itself—a wound closing up, scarring, and disappearing; a sore muscle feeling better; a flu bug that leaves after twenty-four hours. These are examples when your body healed itself without you doing too much to help it (perhaps you gave

> Your body and the environment are in a *constant* state of *exchange*.

it some ice or a Band-Aid). Now consider this—your body also needs to *heal* from its encounter with NBO, but it needs your help this time. NBO has ravaged your body and mind to the point that you need to repair the damage done. Your body has given everything it can to you—performing the thousands of functions it's responsible for at any given second—and you have likely ignored it at best, and hated it at worst. It's time to help your body heal.

We talked a lot in Step 2 about how studies show that merely thinking a thought affects your body's makeup and well-being. Clearly, that's a key part of recovering from NBO—removing the hurtful thoughts and replacing them with positive ones helps you reset your mind and find your inner beauty. Luckily, you can also use the power of your mind to help your body heal itself from the harmful effects of NBO.

How Your Mind Can Heal

We know that our thoughts can improve our outlook and make us feel happier. But can they also *heal* us? Yes! Doctors have studied various methods of healing to prove that point.

The Placebo Effect

One way to show that people's thoughts affect their health is to study the placebo and nocebo effect from medicine. In the placebo effect, a patient receives a bogus treatment, such as a pill without medicine. The patient will usually be unaware that it is a bogus treatment and yet miraculously recover as if he or she had been receiving the medication all along. In the nocebo effect, a patient's condition deteriorates simply because he or she thinks it will.

In *Timeless Healing*, Herbert Benson, MD, discusses the placebo effect, or what he calls "remembered wellness." As part of his research, he reviewed a long history of therapies that were originally designed to alleviate angina pectoris, which is pain in the chest and arms caused by decreased blood flow to the heart. The treatments, such as injections of cobra venom and surgeries to remove the thyroid or parts of the pancreas, were enthusiastically embraced by physicians during the era when they were introduced.

Later, doctors discovered that these methods were completely ineffective. Amazingly, however, when these techniques were used and believed in, they were effective 70 to 90 percent of the time. When physicians began to doubt the efficacy of the treatment, however, their effectiveness dropped to 30 to 40 percent. The belief about whether or not the therapy was effective was a deciding factor in whether or not it was in fact effective.

Recent studies have shown that the placebo effect, or the ability of our beliefs to affect our health and well-being, applies in even extreme cases. A Baylor School of Medicine study evaluating surgery for patients with severe, debilitating knee pain was published in the *New England Journal of Medicine* in 2002. The patients were divided into three groups:

1. In one group, Dr. Bruce Mosely shaved the damaged cartilage in the knee (i.e., he did a little bit of work to improve the knee).
2. In the next group, he flushed out the knee joint, removing material that he thought might be causing the inflammatory effect (i.e., he did a lot of work to improve the knee).

3. The third group received a mock surgery: the patient was sedated, incisions were made, the surgeon talked and acted as if he was conducting the surgery, and after forty minutes the knee was sewn up (i.e., he did nothing to improve the knee).

All three groups received the same postoperative instructions. All three groups improved, and the placebo group improved just as much as the other two groups. In fact, one member of the placebo group who had to walk with a cane before surgery was able to play basketball with his grandchildren afterward! There was absolutely no difference between those who received the surgery and those who didn't.

Placebos are incredibly effective in the treatment of depression. In fact, some studies demonstrate that even when people *know* they are not getting an active drug, the placebo is still effective. Interestingly, antidepressants have performed better and better in clinical trials over the years. According to cell biologist Bruce Lipton, the more the media and advertisements promoted antidepressants, the more effective they became. He explains that beliefs are contagious. Our culture has come to believe, on the whole, that antidepressants work, and they have thus become more effective as this cultural belief has become further solidified. Remember how, in Step 2, we learned that other people's beliefs can profoundly impact you, if you give them the power to do so? There's a perfect example.

Spirituality and Healing from Various Traditions

Numerous scientific studies have consistently confirmed that faith, belief, and spiritual experiences can have a profound impact on healing. Prayer has even been scientifically confirmed as good medicine. Importantly, it doesn't much matter what your particular religious orientation is, for the spiritual underpinnings of healing reach across them all.

In scientific language, this field (that we have been discussing throughout this book) from which we emanate and to which we are connected is non-local, meaning without location. Since we are all connected through this field, healing can occur through prayer and other non-local means of communication. You can not only influence your own health

Healing power is available to you in *every moment*.

through your beliefs, you have the potential to influence *another* person's health and well-being. Here is a small sampling of the many experiments that have confirmed the efficacy of distant healing through prayer, visualization, or non-local intentionality.

Visualizing Cells

Researcher William G. Braud conducted a study at the Mind Science Foundation in San Antonio, Texas, in 1990. Braud tested whether thirty-two unskilled individuals could influence the outcome of red blood cells through visualization. Human red blood cells were placed in a weak salt solution, and each person attempted to stop the cells from swelling and bursting (which would normally result from the saline exposure) by using visualization techniques for ten test tubes. An additional ten test tubes were used as controls. The participants were each shown a color slide of healthy red blood cells to aid in the visualization process. The people conducting the visualization were then placed in separate rooms from the test tubes, and the technicians performing the measurements did not know which tubes were experimental and which ones were controls.

The results were impressive: the red blood cells in the treatment test tubes did not dissolve nearly as much as the controls. In fact, the possibility that these results could have occurred by chance alone was less than one in 5,000.

Using Thoughts to Stimulate Yeast Growth

A 1995 study conducted at the University of Iceland measured the ability of individuals to stimulate the growth of yeast cells in ten test tubes, with ten used as controls. Seven people were involved in the study:

two spiritual healers, one physician who believed in prayer and who used it regularly in his practice, and four students with no experience or interest in healing. After ensuring proper experimental controls, it was found that the treated test tubes did display greater growth. Interestingly, however, the growth was influenced most strongly by the three people who were actively involved in healing. When the scores of the healers were separated out, the odds were less than 2 to 10,000 that the additional growth could have occurred by chance.

Can We Heal Others?

Our ability to influence others non-locally is not limited to test-tube experiments, but applies to human beings as well.

A landmark study on the efficacy of non-local healing or prayer was conducted by cardiologist Randolph C. Byrd in 1988. Byrd's study looked at the efficacy of prayer in the treatment of heart disease. The study involved 393 patients: 192 were prayed for by home prayer groups, while 201 patients did not receive any prayer. The study employed safeguards such as randomization and double-blind controls to help ensure the validity of the results. This means that, to help safeguard against bias and the placebo effect, neither the physicians nor the patients knew who was receiving the treatment—in this case, the prayer.

Your thoughts can help you heal.

The results were staggering, with those receiving prayer benefiting tremendously in the following ways:

1. They were five times less likely to require antibiotics (three patients compared to sixteen).
2. They were three times less likely to develop pulmonary edema, a condition in which the lungs fill with fluid as a consequence of

the failure of the heart to pump properly (six patients compared to eighteen).

3. None of the prayed-for group required endotracheal intubation compared with twelve in the non-prayed-for group.

4. Fewer patients in the prayed-for group died, although the number was not statistically significant.

These findings had a revolutionary impact on the notion of distant healing. Although there were a number of criticisms of the study leveled by skeptics, including lack of data concerning the psychological state of the patients when the study began, the results continue to impact the field of distant or non-local healing.

Another influential study that was done evaluated distant healing in AIDS patients. The study, headed by Elisabeth Targ, a psychiatrist, was a controlled, randomized clinical trial (none of the patients knew whether they were receiving the prayer or not) that used rigorous standards to ensure the accuracy of the results and avoid any of the potential shortcomings of earlier studies. The healers were from varying religious and spiritual backgrounds. A small minority described themselves as religious, while others were trained in nonreligious healing practices. Some worked with people's auras, while others used visualizations or contemplative healing, while others rang bells on behalf of patients to balance their chakras. Still others worked with crystals, chanting, and Qigong. The only criterion in the study was that the healers believed it was going to work.

The results were astounding—after six months researchers found that the treated group was healthier in every parameter. They had significantly fewer doctor visits, fewer hospitalizations, fewer days in the hospital, fewer new AIDS-defining illnesses, and significantly lower severity of the disease. The treatment group also registered significantly improved mood levels on psychological tests.

The results of the AIDS study were further validated by another study that came out one year later from the Mid-America Heart Institute. This study looked at the effect of remote intercessory prayer for hospitalized cardiac patients. In this case those doing the praying were not proclaimed healers. Rather, they needed only to believe in God and the fact that God responds to prayer. The patients who were prayed for showed fewer adverse events and a shorter hospital stay.

Interestingly, it doesn't appear to matter what method is used for healing, so long as an intention is held for the patient to heal. Whether you are invoking the name of Jesus or Buddha, or focusing on rebalancing energy fields and chakras, the key is to have a clear intention for healing and then focusing attention through prayer, chanting, visualization, or other means. Additionally, some of the most effective healers are those who have an ability to get out of the way. They are able to establish their intention and then step back and allow a healing force greater than themselves to flow through them.

Can Healing Others Help You?

What about healing ourselves through helping others? Allan Luks, author of *The Healing Power of Doing Good*, discovered that people who help other people consistently report better health than their peers in any age group. People's health often improved substantially when they began volunteer work. Ninety-five percent of the people Luks surveyed said that helping strangers on a regular, personal basis gave them a pleasurable physical sensation, such as warmth, increased energy, or a sense of euphoria. They also reported greater calm and relaxation. The majority of the volunteers also said that the health benefits returned when they remembered the helping act. According to Herbert Benson, MD, author of *Timeless Healing*, selfless acts of helping others result in improved health, making altruism a viable source for improving your own health and well-being.

Healing and NBO

As you've just read, the latest findings in science and medicine have profound implications for sufferers of Negative Body Obsession. Ask yourself: What are you doing to your body when you are constantly critiquing it for not being thin enough, tall enough, or young enough? Remember, your body is responding to every thought and emotion that you have. When you lambaste it for not fitting into your favorite dress, you are sending it a message. When you are frustrated, angry, depressed, and anxious about your body, you are influencing it at a cellular level in dramatic ways. Like all living things, your body thrives on love, affection, and adoration. It withers in the face of condemnation, critique, and judgment. Learning to love your body not only quiets your mind and calms your emotions; it creates the environment for true healing to occur.

Experience the *majesty* of your own body.

You want to treat your body as you would a baby: with adoration, care, consideration, and unconditional love. If you take a baby and threaten it, criticize it, ignore it, condemn it, and abuse it, you will inflict unimaginable pain, suffering, and damage on that child. On the other hand, when you offer it love and affection, you create an environment for success and well-being. So it is with your body.

In the words of Mahatma Gandhi:

Your beliefs become your thoughts.
Your thoughts become your words.
Your words become your actions.
Your actions become your habits.
Your habits become your values.
Your values become your destiny.

Following are exercises designed to help you love your body and unleash a profound healing force within you so that you can fulfill your destiny and answer your soul's highest calling.

Mindfulness Meditation

Mindfulness meditation is a Buddhist-inspired practice that will help you connect with your body and mind. Many studies document the psychological and physical benefits of mindfulness meditation, helping in areas such as chronic-pain relief and stress reduction. I won't get into them here, but you can check out the appendix for a few books about it.

When applied to Negative Body Obsession and eating disorders, this type of meditation will help you create a "container" for you to process your experiences. If you are in the middle of an intense struggle with an eating disorder, or if you are experiencing intense and overwhelming emotions, mindfulness meditation is a great place to start. Here's what to do:

1. Sit comfortably in a quiet spot and close your eyes. Focus on your breath as you inhale and exhale. As you sit quietly, you will notice that your mind gets pulled away, often forcefully, by a thought in your head, a sound in your environment, an emotion, or a sensation in your body. When your attention gets pulled away, gently let your awareness be with whatever you are experiencing. Then, whenever you feel you are ready, bring your awareness back to your breath. You never want to force or strain; be easy with yourself.
2. You can use this meditation, for example, when you have just binged or eaten unhealthily and are filled with anger, disgust, and frustration. Instead of acting out additional self-destructive behaviors, sit quietly and bring your awareness to your breath. Watch your emotions. Feel the sensations of guilt, anger, shame, frustration, whatever feelings might be arising. Become aware of the thoughts that are moving through your awareness, such as "I am such a slob"; "Why won't anyone help me?"; "I hate myself." Whatever thoughts or emotions you are experiencing, gently let yourself experience them. Then bring your awareness back to your breath.

The Benefits of Mindfulness Meditation

When you become adept at this exercise, you will cultivate the ability to be there for yourself, even in the most difficult of circumstances. You give yourself the time and space to experience negative feelings and emotions, and then let them go. When you are unable to love yourself, you search frantically and aimlessly for someone else to offer you the love and acceptance that you so badly need. Through this simple practice of mindfulness, you can learn how to stop abandoning yourself; you can learn how to support yourself through life's many ups and downs.

This mindfulness practice is also very helpful around food and eating. When you sit down to enjoy a meal, become mindful of the act of eating. Sit quietly with your food, without any distractions such as television or loud music. Bring complete awareness to the process of eating: to holding the utensil in your hand, using it to gather food, placing the food in your mouth, chewing slowly and deliberately, and swallowing. Feel the saliva that is generated in your mouth as you chew and begin to digest your food. Then become aware of the sensations in your body. Bring awareness to how the food feels in your stomach. Notice how your body moves from hunger to satiety.

This simple mindfulness practice will help you become more aware of your physical hunger versus emotional hunger about what and how you eat. This simple act of awareness can enliven and enlarge all aspects of your life.

Bring full awareness to the process of taking a shower and you will experience delightful ecstasy. Bring the power of your attention to eating a single raisin and you will be overwhelmed by the intensity of flavor. Bring your complete attention to another person and you will be astonished by the depth of your interactions. The Buddha taught that this simple practice of mindfulness would lead to enlightenment. Indeed, when you truly practice mindfulness, even the most mundane actions become miracles. It is a powerful practice!

Peace Accord

Negative Body Obsession and eating disorders often revolve around control. Often your mind wants to control your body. But your body, as I have shown, also thinks and feels and has its own agenda. When you attempt to control your body with your mind, your body rebels. Think of your body as a child: if you tell a child that he can't play with a certain toy, *all* he wants to do is play with that one toy. Sure, he might be quiet for a time, but he will rebel and get himself that toy through any means necessary. Your body rebels in the same way—after being told it can't eat, it might binge uncontrollably, or it might rebel in the form of illness, aches, pains, and otherwise poor health. Often people go from being anorexic to eating compulsively. Can you blame their bodies? They've been starved and are fighting for survival and their right to be heard.

Clearly, you've got a war raging inside you. How do you end the war? Broker a peace agreement between the different parts of yourself—mind, body, and spirit.

1. Find a quiet place where you can stand with some space in front of you, behind you, and around you. Close your eyes and picture your spiritual self standing behind you. For the purpose of this exercise, envision your spiritual self as being you at your most radiant and glorious. Where you are standing is your physical body. Standing in front of you is your mind, a combination of your emotions and your intellect. (It's your physical body and mind that are at war.) Envision that your spiritual self is offering you guidance and support while you engage in this dialogue process—think of it as Switzerland!

2. With your eyes still closed, step forward and turn around so that you are facing your physical body. You are now standing in the place of your mind, taking on that persona. Tell your body how you feel about it. Tell your body all the negative thoughts, all the violent thoughts, all

Peace Accord—*continued*

the thoughts you have been silently screaming at it for years. Below is an example. Your dialogue may be more or less intense, depending on where you are in your struggle. The specifics are not important; the goal is simply to adequately express your feelings about your body directly to your body.

I hate you!!! You never do what I want. You are fat and ugly and disgusting. I can't believe I have to live with you! You are an embarrassment, completely despicable. You are so hideous; I can't even believe you are allowed to leave the house. Your thighs are flabby, your stomach is way too large, and I can't even find words to describe your butt. You are worthless! I hate you! You never listen to me; you are constantly getting injured and sick. I want to run and a muscle gets torn; as soon as I start to feel well, you fall sick. I hate you!!!

Don't be embarrassed; don't hold back. This dialogue is one that many of us have had incessantly for years. You are now getting the voice out into the open, to really tell your body in no uncertain terms how you feel about it. Yell, scream. It can even be helpful to get a pillow and imagine that it is your body. Take out all the aggression that you may have toward your body. Attack the pillow with all the vengeance and venom that you may feel toward yourself. Continue this practice until you have nothing more to say to your body.

NOTE: Please be careful not to inflict damage on your physical body during this process.

3. Now take a step backward from where you were originally standing and turn to face your mind, the combination of your emotional and intellectual self. You are now assuming the role of your physical body again.

Peace Accord—*continued*

You are the body that you just screamed at and told off. Now it is your body's turn to tell your intellect and emotional self how it feels.

Shut up and leave me alone!! How dare you stand there and demean me in that way! You are a self-righteous, indignant moron! Yeah, that's right—you heard me. I have worked my butt off (literally) to keep you satisfied. You starve me, and I survive. You stuff me, and I manage to process the food. You critique me with every breath you take; you murmur insults to me; you abuse me, and you misuse me. Yet I am always here. I have never forsaken you. I have never left my post; I have never quit my job. Day in and day out I toil for you. I try whatever new exercise regime you come up with; I try whatever new diet you invent. I have fought endlessly, ceaselessly to keep this ship afloat while you have tried to run us into the shore. You are the one who is inept; you are the one who is an embarrassment. You run me into the ground and then wonder why I need a few days to rest and recuperate. You are insane! You are immature and self-obsessed, a narcissistic egomaniac. You should never have been put in charge of this ship to begin with. You are impossible to satisfy. Get out of here and take your ridiculous, idiotic expectations with you!!!

4. After each side has said everything it can think of, when it has thoroughly run out of insults and anger, check in with your spiritual self who has been quietly standing behind you throughout this process. See if you are ready to make a truce. If both sides are not yet willing to reach a ceasefire, continue going back and forth, embodying your emotional/intellectual self and your body alternately until there is nothing left to say.

Peace Accord—*continued*

5. When they are ready to reach a truce, repeat the following agreement, as if being dictated by your spiritual self:

> *Today we have decided to make a truce. We are calling a cease-fire and are no longer going to live in opposition to one another. Instead, all three of us—emotional self, intellectual self, and body—agree to support and encourage one another. We all surrender to the guidance of our spiritual self. Our spiritual self will now guide us in all endeavors and in all aspects of our life. As a united, integrated being every part will have a voice and will be heard. We commit to this agreement today, vowing to live at peace with one another.*

6. Write this agreement down and sign it three times, one signature each for your emotional/intellectual self, physical self, and spiritual self. Read through this agreement every day, first thing when you wake up, before you go into meditation, and right before you go to bed at night.

Whenever you fall back into the pattern of self-hatred, body criticism, judgment, etc., return to this truce agreement and recommit to living in peace and harmony with all aspects of yourself. The only way forward is through peace and love. If you remain locked in an internal war, you will only inflict harm. Use this agreement to constantly return to peace.

Now that you have established peace within yourself, let's explore a number of activities designed to help you cultivate a better relationship with your body.

Exercise and Physical Movement

You know that NBO has forced you to hate your body instead of love it. Regardless of the form this hatred took—undereating, overeating, hateful thoughts, etc.—it's time to start loving your body in a healthy way. Exercising appropriately is one way to do that.

The evidence on the health benefits of exercise is ubiquitous. Exercise helps in everything from reducing aging to stress management to alleviating depression. You can find thousands of books on exercise, so I won't go into detail here (look for some resources in the appendix, though). What I will do is highlight some of the important points about exercise and physical movement as they relate to Negative Body Obsession.

If you struggle with NBO, chances are you fall into one of two camps: an obsessive overexerciser or an underexerciser. If you are an obsessive overexerciser, you:

- Exercise all the time
- Are filled with fear and anxiety if you miss a day of exercise
- Push yourself constantly and demand a great deal from yourself

The positive is that you enjoy exercise and are aware of the profound health benefits and use it to help manage stress. The negative is that you can push yourself too hard, which often leads to injury instead of health.

On the other hand, if you are an underexerciser, you:

- May dislike physical movement
- Might avoid it at all cost
- Might avoid the gym or going out and exercising because of fear or concern about what other people will think of you

The positive side of underexercising is that you are not driven by a compulsive need to exercise and can often find other ways of soothing yourself and reducing stress. The downside is that you do not experience the benefits of a regular exercise regime.

My personal opinion on this subject is to aim for a healthy mix of activity. Balance will look different for different people, and it will look different during different times in your life. If you like to push yourself, that is perfectly fine, but do it from a place of love, not a place of anxiety. If you don't like to move, opt for something more gentle, and know you don't have to push yourself too hard to achieve profound and lasting health benefits.

Engage a combination of cardiovascular exercise, weight training, and yoga or some form of stretching on a regular basis. Other mind-body techniques, such as Qigong, tai chi, and various forms of martial arts are also useful. Dancing is another great way to exercise if you dislike traditional gym atmospheres.

The best advice is to move and have fun doing it. If you know you have a tendency to overdo and push yourself too intensely, just be aware of this and take it easy once in a while. On the other hand, if you don't push yourself enough, be aware of this and look for opportunities to engage more fully. The best advice is to know yourself and offer yourself whatever you need to move toward greater health and harmony.

Diet

A chapter on befriending your body would not be complete without some discussion of nutrition and a healthy diet. Again, you can find many, many books on nutrition, so I will not go into great detail here. (For further reading, I have included nutrition books in the "Health and Fitness" section of the Resources list.) My intention here, once again, is to highlight some of the key issues unique to Negative Body Obsession.

What we eat is undeniably important to overall health and well-being. Yet, it is equally as important not to stress or worry excessively about what you are eating. Worry and strain can create just as much toxicity as bad food choices. Eating chocolate, for example, can increase your levels of serotonin, a neurotransmitter that gives you an overall feeling of well-being. If, however, you feel guilty about eating the chocolate, you will use up the serotonin that you just produced and thus mitigate the beneficial value of consuming the chocolate.

It is also important not to fool yourself. Use mindfulness meditation as you eat to learn to listen to your body. However, if you have been starving, bingeing, and otherwise interfering with your body's natural hunger and satiety signals, it can be incredibly difficult to listen to your body and decipher any clear message. If you think of yourself as someone who overeats or undereats, it can also skew your ability to listen to your body. As you now know from the intricate relationship between our thoughts and our bodies, we can often convince our bodies that we are hungry or not hungry by virtue of our thoughts.

A Healthy Approach to Eating Well

To help you navigate the often-confusing labyrinth of learning to listen to your body, I offer a two-pronged approach:

1. Practice mindfulness meditation, yoga, exercise, and spending time in nature. Doing so will help you cultivate a more receptive relationship with your body so that you can learn to listen without preconception to what your body may be telling you.
2. Learn everything you can about healthy eating. Read the latest books; listen to the latest audio recordings on healthy diet. Research is constantly being undertaken on this topic; take advantage of it. What we do eat is undeniably as important as what we do not eat. Learn the latest information so you can optimize what you are including and excluding from your diet.

Tailor Your Approach

As I said, no one diet will be appropriate for everyone. For example, I have a client who recently experimented with a raw food diet and found that it dramatically reduced her binge eating. She has struggled with binge eating for almost thirty years and has, for now, found relief in a raw food diet. Yet other people would find a raw food diet much too restrictive and thus detrimental to their overall health.

Remember Your Intentions

Look back at Step 1 and revisit your intention(s) about eating better. Maintain an intention to eat an optimal diet for you, based on your unique desires and preferences, to result in optimal health, and then let the intention go. What you eat will change over time, depending on your moods, the seasons, your relationships, your career, and whatever else may be happening in your life. If you are just stopping self-starvation, you may find yourself eating uncontrollably despite what you know about healthy eating. Allow ups and downs. Be gentle with yourself; be kind to yourself. Simply plant the intention and make a commitment to eat as healthily as you are able.

Laughter

Ah, laughter! Though this book is filled with hope and encouragement, I know we've covered some unhappy topics thus far. This is certainly not one of them! Laughter has far-reaching benefits for the body. Here are some of them:

- Laughter has been shown to reduce levels of stress hormones, such as cortisol, and adrenaline.
- Laughter increases health-enhancing hormones such as endorphins and neurotransmitters.

- Laughter increases antibody-producing cells and enhances the efficiency of T cells, which can result in a stronger immune system.
- Laughter exercises your body. When you laugh, you stretch the muscles throughout your face and body. Your pulse and blood pressure increase, along with the oxygen sent to your tissues. It boosts your heart rate in the same way that exercise does. In fact, a small study was conducted at Vanderbilt University showing that ten to fifteen minutes of laughter burned fifty calories!
- Laughter can help generate positive emotions and manage negative emotions. A good laugh can help you face previously daunting challenges with renewed energy and vigor. It can help you manage the challenges of life and help you find the silver lining in many situations.

But how can you make yourself laugh, especially when it may seem like there is so much to cry about instead? Fortunately, laughter is contagious.

So surround yourself with whatever makes you smile. Listen to comedy shows; watch little kids giggling in the park. Watch videos of people laughing online. Surround yourself with other people's joy and laughter—it will soon have you smiling and laughing, even in the midst of turmoil.

Healing Touch

"Healing touch" is a general term for a wide range of types of skin-to-skin contact used to improve health. The benefits of touch are now widely known—it is effective in everything from helping premature babies develop to reducing stress. The skin is a rich source of hormones as well as immune cells. Touch can release growth hormones into the bloodstream and help with healing on all levels.

Explore the many ways that you can make nurturing touch a bigger part of your life:

- Ayurveda (the ancient medical science from India) encourages giving yourself a daily massage before your shower.
- Indulge yourself with a professional therapeutic massage.
- If you are in a romantic relationship, experiment with loving touch. It could be sexual, but it doesn't need to be. If you are single, give a hug to all of your friends. Hug your children; even hug your pets!

Healing touch is very helpful in overcoming Negative Body Obsession. Touch helps to ground us in our bodies, and can help create a sense of safety and nurturance. It can help us to feel that life is okay, and it can calm the fears that often plague us.

Be sure you feel comfortable with the method you choose, however. Some people with NBO have experienced sexual or physical abuse and many have negative experiences with touch. Make sure that you are very clear about your boundaries and only allow yourself to be touched by anyone in ways that are life-affirming and -enhancing.

Music

Music is a readily accessible art form that has a profound ability to affect your health. Again, don't just take my word for it . . .

Scientific Studies

Dr. Larry Dossey has documented numerous studies demonstrating often miraculous healing from music. Here's an impressive example: Gerry, a sixty-six-year-old man, suffered a brain hemorrhage after diving into a swimming pool in September 1999. He spent five weeks in a coma and later was only able to answer "yes" or "no" to questions. On

December 21, a volunteer choir visited his hospital. As they were singing Christmas carols, Gerry suddenly sat up straight in his bed and began singing Christmas carols with perfect clarity.

Chanting and humming also have therapeutic effects. UCLA researchers discovered that when hospitalized schizophrenics hummed an *mmmmm* sound, they experienced a 60 percent reduction in the overall number of times they had auditory hallucinations. There are also numerous studies documenting angry, stressed, and depressed people finding inner peace and balance through the use of sound.

Music has also been shown to improve surgeons' abilities during surgery, and to bring greater calm and well-being to Alzheimer's patients. Interestingly, doctors in the Department of Psychiatry and Behavioral Sciences at the University of Miami School of Medicine found that the presence of beneficial brain chemicals all increased in the Alzheimer's patients during music treatment. Dr. Ardash Kumar concluded that music therapy can help people maintain hormonal and emotional balance during periods of stress or disease. The effects were so profound that the doctor conducting the study concluded music therapy might be a safer and more effective alternative to conventional medications.

> Your body is a self-prescribing pharmacy.

Using Music in Your Life

As you can probably guess, rapid and intense music will energize you, while calming music will soothe and relax you. Music can also evoke a wide range of emotions. Pick some of your favorite music and listen to it regularly. Set aside some time on a regular basis to listen to music without doing anything else. Simply listen and let your body receive the therapeutic effects. Music can also help manage food cravings. If you feel yourself suffering from an intense food craving, put on some enjoyable music and let it produce the positive experience your body desires.

Find What Works Best for Your Body

Ultimately, the greatest healing will come from your ability to connect with the spiritual domain. When you do that, you'll be more secure in how you are at this exact moment, and you'll be better able to tell what your body needs at any given time.

Certain healing tactics will work for you; others won't. Choose a regimen that works best for you and follow it consistently. Also be willing to change and grow. What works today might be different from what works down the road. Learning to optimize your health is learning how to be adaptable, giving your body what it needs in each moment. You'll want regular healthy interventions to help your body heal from the influence of NBO. Whether your body responds best to exercise, music, or healing touch, give it what it wants for a change. Don't beat it up; don't hate it. Instead, thank it for the amazing work it does on your behalf.

In the words of the great Mahatma Gandhi, "There is a force in the universe, which, if we permit it, will flow through us and provide miraculous results." Permit your body to do its job the way it's meant to be done—with your gratitude and support—and it will give you miraculous results. It will begin to spontaneously heal itself, and you will begin to experience unparalleled energy and vitality.

Points to Remember

- Your physical body is mostly empty space. As you begin to look at your body in this way, you will realize that you have access to a healing and transformational power within yourself in each moment. Your body is not a separate, isolated entity. Rather, it is always connected to the energetic and spiritual domains of which it is a part. Connection with the spiritual domain is your key to health.

- Your body is in a constant state of dynamic exchange and transformation within itself and its environment.
- Our thoughts and beliefs influence our biology.
- The cells in our bodies are themselves thinking entities.
- Engage a combination of these exercises and practices to befriend your body consistently:

  - Practice mindfulness meditation.
  - Regularly review the peace accord you brokered.
  - Exercise and physical movement.
  - Follow a healthy diet.
  - Laugh.
  - Use a healing touch.
  - Listen to music.
  - Rediscover your identity.

CHAPTER TEN

Step 5:
Live Your Purpose

This final step in the five-step process of overcoming Negative Body Obsession provides the emotional passion not only to break free from your obsessions but to live a life that will provide you with more meaning than you ever dreamed possible. This step will shift your experience of life from the limited to the expansive and from the mundane to the miraculous.

You now have the tools you need to achieve this shift. You have learned healthy practices to detach from negative thoughts and create positive ones, and to treat your body with gratitude and care. Once you discover your purpose and begin to live your dreams, you can go on to achieve your highest potential.

Do You Suffer from a Sense of Meaninglessness?

Have you ever asked yourself questions such as: What am I supposed to do? Why am I here on this earth? Why do I have to go through so much suffering and pain? Why was I born? Wouldn't it be easier to not exist at all?

If you have, you're not alone. Depression, anxiety, and obsessive behavior are rampant in today's culture. One out of every five women in the United States is on an antidepressant! Afraid that our lives have no purpose, we wonder why we are here on this earth in the first place.

Why are we so empty inside? When you are disconnected from your Source, you are also disconnected from your sense of purpose—that's why a feeling of meaninglessness is common among people with NBO. No matter what you try to achieve in the physical world—riches, a beautiful body, a loving relationship—you can't ignore the human need to fulfill a sense of purpose. In the words of the great philosopher Nietzsche, "He who has a Why to live for can bear almost any How." NBO has buried your Why under those negative thoughts and insecurities. You need to relocate your Why and fulfill it, overcoming any obstacles that How throws your way using the techniques you've learned in this book.

The Benefits of Living with Purpose

You've probably figured out my pattern by now—I explain something, then convince you it's true by backing up the theory with research. Here are some interesting facts about how much healthier it is to live with a sense of purpose. Numerous studies have shown that people who have a sense of purpose have better health, better relationships, and a higher overall sense of well-being. Without this sense of purpose, people are more likely to suffer from anxiety and depression, as well as Negative Body Obsession.

Sandor Ferecnzi, a psychoanalyst in the early 1900s, found that anxiety and depression occurred more often on Sundays than on any other day of the week. Why? People were dreading going back to work on Monday. Other studies have shown that more heart attacks occur on Mondays than any other day. Why? Likely because the stress of going back to work finally became too much for people's hearts. When your work feels meaningless, it can be quite literally unbearable. On the other hand, work can also cover up an underlying sense of apathy and futility in life. Vacations and retirement have been shown to produce anxiety and depression in some people—even though they should be times to be enjoyed! Why? The reason may be that in many cases people's work provides them with a sense of purpose, but this purpose doesn't extend to the rest of their lives. When they retire or go on vacation, their underlying sense of meaninglessness is exposed.

The Importance of Purpose in Life-or-Death Situations

At its most basic level, purpose can literally help people stay alive. While this may seem far from our discussion of NBO, it unfortunately is not. As those of you suffering from eating disorders or intense emotional struggles probably know, continued abuse of your body and mind can lead to precarious life-and-death situations. Finding a sense of purpose, however, helps those stuck in these very dark and horrific places, as the following studies show.

Purpose and Suicide

Researchers at New York State Psychiatric Institute investigated the role of living with a purpose in the suicide attempts of depressed psychiatric patients. They studied eighty-four people suffering major depression, trying to determine why thirty-nine of them had never attempted to kill themselves. Their research showed that not having a reason to live was the key predictor. The depressed patients who perceived life as having more meaning were less likely to kill themselves, even with intense, overwhelming depression.

In another "study" of sorts, written up in his book *Man's Search for Meaning*, psychiatrist Viktor Frankl highlights the importance of meaning for survival under the worst imaginable circumstances. He writes that meaning was essential for surviving one of the most horrific events in human history, the Holocaust. Frankl himself survived the Nazi concentration camps, but lost his wife, his brother, both parents, and every possession he had ever owned, including a prized manuscript he was writing. Though his situation was dire, he managed to find a reason to live. While in the concentration camps, he decided that one concrete way he could live his purpose was to prevent his fellow prisoners from committing suicide. As a trained psychiatrist, he was uniquely positioned to carry out this task, since his fellow inmates would often confide in him.

He tells the story of two men who, at two different times, told him that they had decided to commit suicide. They gave the same reason: they had nothing more to expect from life. They were doomed to a life of endless suffering, starvation, torture, and eventually the gas chamber.

"In both cases," writes Frankl, "it was a question of getting them to realize that life was still expecting something from them; something in the future was expected of them." One man was a scientist who had written several volumes of a book. It was incomplete, however, and he was the only person who could finish it. The other man had a child in another country waiting for him. The book implies that both men decided against suicide. Frankl discovered that a person would not commit suicide once he or she realized his or her specific obligation in life—*that life expected something of them.*

Other Benefits of Purpose

Another study conducted at the University of Florida Institute of Aging shows that people who have a feeling of purpose in life are more likely to experience a general sense of well-being, exhibit fewer depressive symptoms, and have a decreased fear of death.

Other studies too numerous to mention show that people with a sense of purpose have a tendency to weigh less, have lower levels of inflammation, better sleep patterns, lower blood-sugar levels, and higher levels of good cholesterol. Dr. Ann Vincent, a physician and clinical researcher at the Mayo Clinic, says that people with high self-esteem, who are optimistic, and who have a sense of meaning and purpose, have better physical health.

The bottom line: I cannot overstate the importance of knowing and living your sense of purpose.

What Does It Mean to Live Your Purpose?

Even if you are not sure exactly what it is at the moment, you are here on purpose and for a purpose. Your existence is not random; it was intended. Before you were even born, you were intended. Everything that is created begins with an intention, and your existence is no different. You were intended to realize your soul's highest potential.

What you do to earn money is just one expression of living your purpose. In reality, your purpose is much broader than what you do—it is who you are. Living your purpose is about discovering who you truly are. Once you discover this, you will begin to do things with your life that are an expression of this newfound identity. You will find yourself sharing your own abundance with others. Expressing your unique gifts and talents in service to others is a limitless source of ongoing inspiration. Deepak Chopra puts it this way: "Everyone has a purpose in life . . . a unique gift or special talent to give to others. And when we blend this unique talent with service to others, we experience the ecstasy and exultation of our own spirit, which is the goal of all goals."

As you live from this place, your life will be spontaneously imbued with meaning on an ongoing and increasingly constant basis.

Ask yourself: How can I *help*? How can I *serve*?

One of the most liberating discoveries you can make as you proceed down this path of living on purpose and in purpose is to realize that you are in the driver's seat. Your life is the result of the choices that you have made in the past; it is the result of the intentions that you had in the past, whether you were conscious of them or not. If you want to create a different life with different results, begin by making different choices. Different choices will produce different results. In the famous words of Albert Einstein, "Insanity is doing the same thing over and over again and expecting a different result." As you become a conscious creator, you can act in different ways and generate different results.

You Are a Creator

Try this thought experiment. Sit in a quiet, comfortable place and imagine the following:

1. Assume that before you were ever born, you intended to manifest in this particular time, in this particular body, to accomplish your specific purpose. Assume that you chose your parents, you chose your situation, you chose your body, and you chose your purpose. You chose your challenges. You chose your strengths as well as your weaknesses, and you chose them for a specific reason. Ask yourself: How does this change my perception of my past? My family? My successes? My failures?
2. Then assume that nothing is random; nothing is without reason. You might not know the reason at the time that it occurs, but there is one. When life seems to go your way, there is a reason. When life seems to not go your way, there is a reason. Can you think of any time where after a seemingly bad event occurred, you realized there was a reason it happened the way it did?
3. Consider that everything you have ever experienced, every strength you have, every weakness, every challenge, and every triumph, can be used to serve other people; it can be used to help you live your purpose. Try to think of ways you could share your experiences and talents with others right now.
4. Shift your mindset away from being the victim of anything to being the creator of it. (This does not mean you are in denial or masochistic. Certainly, many of us undergo intense abuse or other heartbreaking experiences, and it is never desirable to suffer unnecessarily.) When we identify as the victim, however, we give someone else our power. When we discover that we are the creator, we realize that we can choose how to respond in any situation. If we cannot change the situation itself, we can change our response to it. This is not always easy, but it is the key

You Are a Creator—*continued*

to living a happy and successful life. Ask yourself if there are areas of your life you are letting someone else control. Can you change who's in charge?

Find Your Intense Emotion and Burning Desire

An ancient Indian text, the Brihadaranyaka Upanishad, states (verse IV.4.5):

> *You are what your deep, driving desire is.*
> *As your desire is, so is your will.*
> *As is your will, so is your deed.*
> *As is your deed, so is your destiny.*

One great way to identify your "desire" is to become aware of what evokes intense emotion in you. What have you experienced that creates passion or desire? It can be both pleasurable and painful. Did you always want to do something but didn't think you were beautiful enough? Did your dreams get sabotaged by your hating your body? Are you simply bored and not sure what you want? Do you feel like you are lacking something in your life? Jot down some notes and see if anything jumps out at you. All of these feelings can be clues to help you discover your purpose.

Choosing a New Life

It's true: there are many reasons why you have struggled and suffered. As you discovered in Step 2, your parents probably could have done things differently; your teachers could have done things differently; society could have done things differently. But whatever happened has happened and is in the past. Once you have detached from these negative influences, you must live as if you are the creator of your life. As the creator, you always have a choice about how you will respond.

In his book, *The Success Principles*, Jack Canfield gives an equation to explain this truth: E + R = O; Event + Response = Outcome. This equation shows that you have a choice:

1. You can blame events in your life as the cause of your suffering and challenges. This choice is disempowering because events are sometimes outside of your direct and immediate control.
2. Or, you can change your response in order to yield a different outcome. When you focus on your response to life, you can make choices that will move your life in the direction that you want it to go.

Sometimes, however, you may find it difficult to make different choices. You will find yourself driven by the compulsions and obsessions that NBO puts in your mind. You *want* to make different choices but seem unable to control what you do. This behavior is particularly prevalent in people who have eating disorders and/or Negative Body Obsession. However, as you practice meditation on a regular basis, as you become mindful, as you reduce your stress, as you complete the exercises in this book, you will notice that these obsessive behaviors begin to diminish. Your awareness outside of these compulsions will expand and you will discover your ability to make different choices that will yield different results.

By focusing on your response to events or situations, you will become aware of your thoughts, your emotions, your dreams, your energy, and your behavior. It is through becoming conscious that you can change.

Almost miraculously, you will find that as you change your response to events, the events themselves seem to change. Once you learn to respond differently to life, you will actually begin to create a different life.

Knowing Your Purpose Can Help You Out of NBO

It's especially important to discover your purpose, because it can be a path away from NBO. My client Fon's story helps illustrate this point.

Fon's Story

Consider the example of my clients from Thailand (I have edited her writing for clarity). Fon is a twenty-two-year-old woman in Thailand and has been struggling with bulimia for six years. This is the correspondence she sent when she first contacted me:

I have suffered from bulimia for six years and it still continues, like a circle I can never ever escape. I can't finish my diploma because of this illness; it steals everything from me. I still have negative food thoughts; I restrict myself. I know what is good for me and what isn't. I can't get rid of this thought and I have Negative Body Thoughts about my round face and big belly sometimes.

I am really interested in this field too. I want to recover and help others who suffered like me. I have read about your experiences and I admire you. It's terrific because finally you got through it and now you offer to help others.

In Thailand, we have more than 300,000 people suffering from eating disorders but there are no specialists who understand us. Yes, we have many psychiatrists, and some psychologists and some hypnotherapists, but none of them ever experienced NBO themselves so they don't know how hard it is to conquer this problem.

I have seen many psychiatrists and one hypnotherapist yet my health has not improved. I became the new case-study in a hospital; they wanted to learn from me. All they can give me are many instructions I can't follow. Too few people understand this torment; you are right! Bulimia stole my life, my friends, my energy, my self-respect—everything.

My family—they seem to understand but actually they can't accept the truth. They pretend there's nothing abnormal. They act like I am ok but I know they are too ashamed of me or try to hide their pain. I understand them but it make me quite sad.

I don't know where to turn to; I really appreciate your help. My strong intention is to overcome this illness and then I will go back to studying. I want to help other sufferers, too.

Even in the midst of intense suffering, Fon knows her desires. She wants to return to school to finish her degree, and she also wants to help other people heal once she has healed herself. As she increases in strength and conquers the demons that plague her, she will be able to live her purpose. The intensity of her pain fuels her desire to help other people. Again, it is never desirable that anyone should suffer, but you always have a choice about how you respond to your suffering. Changing your response can facilitate your healing and your ultimate freedom.

Give and You Shall Receive

Yet another benefit of knowing your purpose is that when you act on it, you not only serve others, but you continue to heal yourself as well. It is the law of reciprocation at work: when you give healing, you will receive healing. When you serve from the heart, you will receive back tenfold.

Let me underscore this point: if you feel an intense need for something, consider that you might want to create it so that you can give it away. What does this mean? Consider these examples:

- If you want love, give love.
- If you want someone to understand your pain, understand someone else's pain.
- If you want to feel supported and nurtured, learn to support and nurture others.

This is not, however, an invitation to stay in destructive relationships in any way, shape, or form. If the relationships you are currently in are not offering you the support you need, cultivate other relationships that will give you what you need. If you give and don't receive anything in return, you should evaluate the relationship to be sure it's healthy and enriching. It does not do any good to give to the point of depleting yourself and diminishing your well-being. We'll discuss relationships in greater detail in the following chapter, but for now, just know that it is important that you surround yourself with nurturing relationships, and if that means letting go of some of your current social involvements, that is okay.

Linda's Success Story

Living with purpose can help you overcome NBO, as you experience greater and greater fulfillment in your life. Take, for example, one of my clients mentioned earlier, Linda. When we began working together, Linda hated her job. She worked as an administrative assistant and found her job to be boring, frustrating, and dissatisfying. She would come home from work at night and find herself eating compulsively. She would then condemn and chastise herself for overeating.

Ask the Universe

Get in the habit of trusting that the universe will provide you with answers if you ask the questions. As you have learned, you are in charge of your life and you have a purpose to fulfill. Consider this quote from Wayne Dyer:

> That inner being-ness knows why you're here, but your ego prods you to chase after money, prestige, popularity, and sensory pleasures and miss the purpose of living . . . focusing on the demands of the ego leaves you feeling unfulfilled. Deep within you, at the level of your being, is what you were intended to become, to accomplish, and to be. In that inner placeless place, you're connected to the power of intention. It will find you. Make a conscious effort to contact it and listen. Practice being what you are at the source of your soul. Go to your soul level, where intention and purpose fit together so perfectly that you achieve the epiphany of simply knowing this is it.

In this exercise, you're going to contact the universe and listen to what it tells you. The universe will not only provide you with the information you need to discover your purpose, it will also provide you with the tools you need to live your purpose and to manifest whatever you want and need. The universe has no limits; it has no scarcity; it is unlimited potential and pure abundance. When you align yourself with the creative energy of the universe, it will answer your questions and provide you with whatever you desire, the only caveat being that you are dedicated to serving and helping others through what you say, have, and do.

Ask the Universe—*continued*

In earlier chapters, you learned the importance of meditation. When you sit down to meditate, before you begin, ask yourself the following questions:

- Who am I?
- What do I want?
- What is my purpose in life? How can I help? How can I serve?

Ask yourself these questions every morning and every evening before you go into meditation. Write them down on a piece of paper and read them out loud before you begin.

When you come out of meditation, visualize what you would feel like if you were living on purpose. Assume that you are already living your purpose. Assume that you are filled with unwavering dedication and unsurpassable inspiration. What does this feel like in your body? Take a few minutes after you finish your meditation, before you open your eyes, visualizing what living on purpose and with purpose would feel like for you.

Trust that the universe will answer your questions. Be on the lookout for answers; they may come in ways you hadn't imagined. Finding your purpose sometimes simply entails becoming increasingly aware of opportunities that present themselves. It might not be a huge change or shift, such as a new career. It might simply be doing whatever you are currently doing with a sense of purpose, knowing that you are here for a reason, fulfilling what you were meant to fulfill.

On the other hand, living with purpose might mean a dramatic shift in your life. Simply stay alert, stay aware, stay open.

After we worked together for about six months (using the steps you're learning), she began studying to become a librarian. She had an extremely busy schedule, working while going to school. During one of our conversations, however, she mentioned that she felt more like she was living with purpose. She said the library of science program "brings me alive" and is "an expression of me." She mentioned feeling a sense of contentment, being filled with satisfaction, knowing that she was doing something to live more on purpose. This led to a dramatic decrease in her compulsive evening eating. She explained that it helped having a "healthy focus outside of myself" that uses her unique talents and creativity. She also said that it helped being involved with like-minded people.

> You are here *on* purpose and *for* a purpose.

The connection between NBO and purpose is undeniable. Find your purpose—as Linda did—and enjoy the benefits.

You May Share Your Hero's Traits

When you are attracted to someone or something, it is often because you already have these qualities but want more of them. Often, the people you are most attracted to reveal something about your own purpose. You are attracted to them precisely because they reflect your own greatness. Use this attraction to further cultivate the qualities you admire within yourself.

Setting and Managing Goals

People with goals are among the most productive and successful in every area of their lives. Goals help to provide direction for your life; they can work as an internal compass. It is important, however, not to let yourself become overwhelmed. Don't feel like you have to accomplish everything immediately. Set the goals; read them before you go into your meditation; visualize your life when you come out of meditation. Then just let everything go. Release it and let the universe work out the details; there is no reason for effort or strain. Simply stay on the lookout for how help shows up in your life.

Pick Your Heroes

Another way to uncover your purpose is to identify people who inspire you. This person or people might be someone you know personally, such as your high school math teacher, or someone who is a legend, such as Mother Teresa or Nelson Mandela. Think back over the emotional experiences you have had and the people who have evoked your admiration. Even events in your childhood can point in the direction of your purpose. The key is to find people who touch your heart and awaken your desire to live for something greater than yourself.

This exercise relates to the previous one. Ask yourself the following questions:

- Which people evoke a sense of passion and purpose in me?
- Who do I want to emulate?
- Who do I admire?
- Who are my heroes?

If you are not sure, pick a few well-known figures from history and read about them or watch movies about them. Search them out and see what resonates in your heart.

Envision Your Power

As we've discussed, what you think becomes your reality. In this exercise, take time to envision what you want your life to look like. What is your vision for your health? Your work and career? Your finances? Your friendships and romantic relationships? Your personal growth? Your recreation and free time? Your contribution to the community? What do you want from life, and what do you want to give back to life? Remember, the universe operates on the principle of exchange. If you want to get much from life, give much to life. Give abundantly and the universe will give the same to you.

Get a piece of paper and a pen. Write out your ideal vision for your life in each of the categories listed above. When we struggle with Negative Body Obsession, our visions are often eclipsed by a focus on our bodies. Take the time to imagine what you want the rest of your life to look like. Don't impose any limits on yourself—create a vision that truly excites you. What dreams do you have that will make you jump out of bed in the morning and drive you passionately throughout your day? What enlivens your heart and touches your soul enough to help you persist in the face of any challenge? Release any self-imposed limitations and begin to dream.

Without a vision, you have no idea where you are going. When you create a vision that excites you, you are endowing your life with focus and energy. You are beginning the process of creating a life that you truly love; it all begins with a dream.

In part, your vision represents your intention for how your purpose will unfold and manifest in your life. For example, say you define your purpose as "helping others experience more joy and laughter in their lives." Your vision might be to learn the funniest jokes around and tell them to your friends and family during the holiday. Perhaps your vision includes attending comedy clubs to bring more humor into your own life that you can share with others. Maybe your vision is to become a comedian yourself. Your vision can be as grand or as simple as you wish; just listen to your own heart. Your vision will also include other areas of your life that might not seem directly related to your purpose. Over time, however, you will come to see how it is all intertwined and related.

Create a Vision Board

Once you have written out the vision for your life, put your vision into pictures. Create a "vision board" for your life. Fill your vision board with materials that inspire you. Use photos of your heroes, your favorite quotes, pictures of nature, artwork. Use anything and everything that reminds you of your vision and your dreams.

Take the time to create a vision board—it will move you in the direction you want to go. Read through your vision and look at it every day before you go into meditation and when you come out of meditation. Look at it and read it periodically throughout the day. It will energize you when you are tired and motivate you when you encounter challenges. If your vision doesn't excite you, change it until it does.

Set Goals

Once you have developed a vision and created your vision board, break your vision down into specific goals. Your *vision* is your inspirational powerhouse; it gives you the emotional fuel you need to fulfill it. Your *goals* are the specific actions to move you in the direction of your vision.

For example, let's assume that part of your vision is to achieve a healthy body weight and a peaceful, easy relationship with food and your body. What would this mean in concrete terms? Would it mean that you eat when you are hungry and stop when you are full? Would it mean that you learn to have a healthy, balanced, exercise regime? Set specific goals for your vision. Don't worry too much about the details; this should be fun and not overwhelming. Take the time to write down your specific goals on a piece of paper.

Once you have your goals, read through them before you go into your meditation. Then pay attention to see how your goals are being fulfilled. Here is an example of how this whole process might play out:

Using the example above, let's say that part of your vision is to achieve a healthy, comfortable body weight and a peaceful, easy relationship with food and your body. Your goal is to eat when you are genuinely hungry and stop when you are full, not stuffed. This is a challenge for you because you have a tendency to eat emotionally, or perhaps you are a compulsive eater recovering from anorexia. You read this goal, along with others, before your meditation. Within a few weeks, you purchase a book that talks about how brain chemicals can influence our hunger and satiety levels. You learn about certain foods you can eat to help curb cravings, or perhaps you learn a technique for managing uncomfortable emotions.

Celebration Party

Just as laughter is good medicine, a party is incredible therapy. You have done the work:

- You set an intention; you identified and detached from your negative thoughts.
- You are discovering who you really are and are befriending your body.
- You are committed to uncovering and living your purpose.
- You have discovered that you are beautiful; you are desirable, and you are imminently worthwhile.

Wow! Talk about a transformation. Now it's time to celebrate the new You, the You that you have always been but never knew; the You whom you have longed for; the You who has been hidden there all along.

If you have supportive friends, have them all over for a grand party. Invite anyone who has been a positive part of your journey. Ask if anyone wants to commit to a new and higher vision of themselves. You can hold each other accountable.

If you don't have any friends who can come, or if your Negative Body Obsession has been a secret, celebrate in a private way that is meaningful to you.

You are a legend in the making; celebrate your victory!

Points to Remember

- You are here on purpose and for a purpose.
- Living on purpose has a positive effect on health and well-being.
- Your purpose is not only what you do—it is who you are.
- You have the ability to control your decisions and create the life you want.
- Use these exercises to help you discover your purpose:

  - Assume that everything in your life has happened for a reason.
  - Become a conscious creator by changing your response to situations to produce different results.
  - Become aware of what creates passion and desire within you.
  - Ask the universe for help.
  - Pick your heroes.
  - Envision yourself living with purpose.
  - Set goals to move you forward.
  - Have a party to celebrate your success!

Part III

Nurturing Relationships

CHAPTER ELEVEN

Overcoming Negative Body Obsession While in a Relationship

Even though the tools you learned in Parts I and II of this book have given you support for overcoming Negative Body Obsession, don't worry if you continue to experience symptoms for some time. Luckily, the exercises and activities you've completed (as well as what you'll read in the next chapter) will help you during tough times. One particular area you may still find difficult to manage is your relationships with family, friends, or significant others.

You've already read about how NBO can seduce you into isolation or it can compel you to enter into unbalanced relationships in a futile attempt to find solace from anxiety and pain. Once in a relationship, NBO can make it impossible to create a harmonious, peaceful connection.

Fortunately, when you break the stranglehold NBO has on your life, you can develop the kinds of relationships that will increase both your joy and your success in life.

The Power of Relationships on Health

Experiencing love, intimacy, and connection plays an integral role in health and well-being. Here is some of the research on the impact of relationships and healing. Studies consistently show that anything promoting love and intimacy has the ability to heal, while anything promoting isolation, separation, loneliness, and alienation often leads to disease and even premature death.

Strong Relationships and Healthy Bodies

In his beautiful book, *The Healing Power of Intimacy*, Dr. Dean Ornish explains that nurturing relationships and feelings of love are protective and can actually make the immune system stronger. Conversely, feelings of isolation and loneliness create a fertile environment for disease and discomfort to grow.

Harvard University conducted a study of 126 healthy students in the 1950s. They were each given a questionnaire to measure how they felt about their parents. Thirty-five years later, medical records were obtained on the study participants and detailed medical and psychological histories were taken. Here's what they found:

- A full 91 percent of participants who said they did not have a warm relationship with their mothers when they first completed the questionnaire had been diagnosed with serious diseases in midlife. Yet only 45 percent of participants who believed they had warm relationships with their mothers had been diagnosed with serious diseases.
- About 82 percent of participants who registered low warmth and closeness with their fathers had diagnosed diseases in midlife, contrasted with only 50 percent of those who had high warmth and closeness.
- 100 percent of the participants who had relationships low in warmth and closeness with both parents had diseases in midlife, contrasted with only 47 percent of those who indicated high levels of closeness with their parents.

This study does not mean that people who do not have close relationships with their parents are doomed to ill health. One of the reasons that early relationships are indicative of future health or illness is the patterns of relating that get developed in early childhood. If your family was not particularly close, you can still learn new ways of relating that increase intimacy in your life with health-enhancing benefits.

Social Interaction and Health

Other studies have investigated how loneliness affects health. For example, in 1965, the California Department of Health Services began studying approximately 7,000 men and women. They found that study participants who lacked social and community ties were about two to three times more likely to die during the nine-year follow-up period. The link between social isolation and premature death was found to be a more powerful predictor of health and longevity than age, gender, race, socioeconomic status, self-reported physical health, smoking, alcoholic beverage consumption, overeating, or physical activity! People with close social ties and unhealthy behaviors actually lived longer than those with poor social ties and healthier behaviors. Of course, people with both close social ties and healthy behaviors lived the longest.

You can begin to live the *life of your dreams* beginning today.

Relationships and Healing

In 1989, David Spiegel and colleagues at Stanford Medical School published their study findings about healing and relationships in *The Lancet*, a British journal. They had observed two groups of women with metastatic breast cancer. Both groups received conventional medical care, including chemotherapy, surgery, radiation, and medications. One group also met together for an hour and a half once a week for one year. The group members came together and shared how they felt about the illness and how it was affecting their lives. (The group was led by a therapist who had breast cancer in remission.) Over time, the group developed a strong sense of community and connection. A later study published in 2001 in the *New England Journal of Medicine* found that although the patients survived for about the same length of time whether or not they were in a support group, simply *being* in the support group improved participants' mood and pain.

You are worthy of *love* exactly as you are *right now*.

In another study, Dr. Sheldon Cohen and colleagues at Carnegie-Mellon University and the University of Pittsburgh tested 276 healthy volunteers ranging from eighteen to fifty-five years old. They were all given nasal drops containing a virus that causes the common cold. The researchers then assessed how much participation each volunteer had in twelve types of social relationships, including spouses, parents, in-laws, children, neighbors, friends, workmates, schoolmates, and others.

Although almost all people exposed to the virus technically became infected, not everyone developed the signs and symptoms of a cold. The number of social relationships seemed to help people who were infected from actually developing a cold. People reporting only one to three types of relationships had more than four times the risk of developing a cold than those with six or more types of relationships.

What Does It Mean for Those with NBO?

This research has profound implications for anyone struggling with Negative Body Obsession or disordered eating. Why? Because as we have already discussed, NBO thrives on isolation. It tells you that you are not good enough, beautiful enough, young enough, or thin enough to feel loved, nurtured, and cherished. Likewise, eating-disordered behavior thrives in secrecy. Many struggle silently with bulimia or binge eating for years, with even their closest family members unaware of their struggle. The cycle of embarrassment, shame, and insecurity feeds on itself, creating more pain and suffering.

The lesson of these studies is that it's vital that you create healthy relationships in order to enjoy optimal health. Though NBO might try to pull you into isolation or dysfunctional relationships, resist and find joy in healthy interactions of all sorts. This chapter will help you understand how NBO affects relationships so you can be aware of its influence and begin to change it.

The Myths That NBO Perpetuates

In order to reduce the influence of NBO in your relationships, you must understand exactly how NBO affects them. You must understand the lies it tells and expose the myths it wants you to believe. This chapter will help you expose NBO's myths so you can be aware of them and work to erase them from your life.

NBO Myth #1: I must isolate myself from people because the only thing that matters is how I look.

Behind the development of NBO is the subtle yet gnawing fear that you are not good enough. When you become concerned that you are not popular enough or beautiful enough or lovable enough, NBO steps in to "save the day." It convinces you that your real problem is that you're just too fat and ugly. If you only looked different, everything else would fall into place: you'd be okay.

NBO gives you a simple way to approach the world, and a simple way to measure your success or failure. NBO consumes all your time and energy and convinces you that you are not quite good enough to be socializing with others. As you became more obsessed *Love* and *nurturance* are your *birthright.* with how you look, you probably became less social, gradually but noticeably lessening the time you spend with family and friends while increasing the amount of time you spend by yourself. NBO's first and most damaging strategy is to isolate you from your friends and loved ones.

NBO offers up a series of lies that perpetuate Myth #1. The lies sound something like this:

- When you are beautiful, you will be happy.
- You will have meaningful friendships and lasting relationships only if you are perfect.
- When you are thin and beautiful, you will be worthy of love and affection.
- When you are attractive enough, you will be successful.
- When you conform to society's ideals of beauty, you will feel good about yourself.
- When you are toned, fit, and beautiful, you will be able to live the life you want.
- You need to be perfect in order to be loved.

You can write down your own version of NBO's lies; yours may sound a little different. The fact is, they are lies. They are particularly insidious because society reinforces many of these lies. Our culture teaches us that happiness is something we achieve when we acquire whatever we desire. In reality, happiness does not begin when something else is achieved; it is the starting point from which success can flower. The truth of the matter is:

- You are worthy of love and affection simply because you exist. Love and nurturance are your birthright.
- When you love and accept yourself, you can be successful regardless of your body weight or your appearance.
- When you love and accept yourself, you can make choices that will lead you to find and maintain a healthy body weight.
- When you love and accept yourself, you can enter into fulfilling and lasting relationships.

- You can begin to live the life you want right now; you can begin to take steps to make it happen.

Don't let NBO seduce you into isolation and loneliness. Reread the truths listed above and remind yourself that you deserve healthy, loving relationships just as you are right now.

NBO Myth #2: I need someone else to make me feel beautiful, safe, and good about myself.

NBO preys on your insecurity and reinforces it endlessly. Because you can never be thin enough or perfect enough to satisfy the voices inside your head, you begin to feel that you'll never be loved. In an attempt to ease this angst, you may search for acceptance from others.

When I was caught in the early stages of NBO, I threw myself into the arms of men hoping to find in them the love and acceptance I couldn't give myself. I believed subconsciously that if only I could be loved and cared for by someone else, I would be able to accept myself. I put myself into dangerous situations, risking my health and my safety in a hopeless attempt to find love. My story may sound familiar to many of you.

Here are some of the lies that NBO uses to perpetuate Myth #2:

- If someone else thinks you are beautiful, you will think you are beautiful.
- You need to use your sexuality to be loved.
- If you are with the right person, everything will be okay.
- You can't stand up for yourself because that might end your relationship.
- If you aren't perfect, you won't be worthy of love.
- You must be thin in order to be desirable.

You may not even be aware that you are operating under these lies. Step back and objectively evaluate your behavior in relationships to see if the lies are affecting you. Here is a hint: if your relationships are characterized by angst, frustration, and pain, you are probably operating under some lies. As you debunk the lies, replace them with the following truths:

- When you see the beauty in yourself, other people will see that beauty as well.
- Your sexuality is a gift that you can only truly enjoy when you are living with a sense of abundance and self-acceptance.
- There's no perfect person who can silence the harsh voices inside your head and make everything okay.
- You can create boundaries to keep yourself safe and state clearly what you want from a relationship.
- Being alone can be an important step of growth and you should never stay with someone out of need.
- You are worthy of love exactly as you are, right now, in this very moment.
- Any relationship worth having is not defined by your body or your weight.

Searching for happiness by running after relationships only leads to pain and weakness because you give other people the power to determine your feelings. You set yourself up as an object, and then look to others to make you feel worthwhile.

It's true, of course, that other people can and do affect the way you feel about yourself. Parents, partners, and friends can give you a sense of safety and well-being; they can help to soften the edges of life's challenges. But they can also sap your creativity, strength, energy, and enthusiasm if they are exacerbating NBO in your life. This is why it is so important that you choose carefully who you spend time with.

You are responsible for your *self-esteem* and *self-respect*.

If you are operating under NBO's myths and lies, chances are you are feeling insecure or unlovable. And when you search for a relationship from this place of inadequacy, you're going to run into trouble. When you need someone to make you feel okay about yourself, you are more willing to compromise yourself and your well-being for the relationship. You might end up in relationships with people who take advantage of you. Or you might end up with people who take care of you at the price of your independence and self-esteem. When you come from a place of abundance and self-acceptance, however, you can make good decisions about the relationships you want in your life.

NBO Myth #3: I can have a successful relationship with a significant other even if I have NBO.

Sorry, this is a myth. Here's what happens: You and your partner think you are falling in love with one another. You experience romance and excitement and all those wonderful early-relationship joys. Over time, however, you come to find that there's an unwelcome third wheel in your relationship: NBO. And guess what? NBO is a jealous and self-interested companion. It wants all your attention; it has no interest in additional companionship.

You may have already found that NBO makes it virtually impossible to have a long-term committed relationship. Have you ever gone out to a romantic dinner with your sweetheart only to become gripped by the fear that you'd eaten too much and would gain weight? When you take your clothes off, are you afraid of looking fat and ugly? Instead of being able to focus on sex, are you worried about how your thighs look at a particular angle? Do you compulsively ask your partner whether or not you have gained weight? These are just some of the ways that NBO puts an enormous strain on your relationships.

The more *closely* you voice your needs, the *greater* your chance of having them met.

You may have experienced fears similar to these, or you may have your own version of how NBO affects your relationships. But here are a number of common lies:

- There's nothing wrong with living with NBO.
- You can have a loving relationship even while listening to the voices of NBO.
- It is your partner's job to make you feel self-assured.
- Your issues don't create tremendous strain on a relationship.
- The relationship can and will make NBO go away.

The truth is more like this:

- Depending on the severity of your NBO, you are struggling with a variety of issues that you need to deal with before you can have a happy relationship.
- You cannot be fully available for intimacy and connection while listening to the voices of NBO.
- You are the one who is responsible for your self-esteem and self-respect.
- You also must take responsibility for dealing with your NBO. Supportive relationships can help, but only you can free yourself from it.

The bottom line: you can't sweep NBO under the rug or hope that a relationship will solve it. Only through self-inquiry and self-discovery will you be able to overcome it.

NBO Myth #4: If I can fully control someone else, I will be safe.

NBO can also convince you that if you can control other people, you will feel good about yourself. If you find that you *can't* control the people and events of your life, you may be overcome by feelings of frustration, insecurity, and anxiety. For example, do you ever try to control what your significant other eats or drinks? Be honest with yourself. What about subtly (or not-so-subtly) trying to control how your partner spends his time, what he does, where he goes, etc. No wonder NBO makes it difficult to experience a loving relationship! Don't be too hard on yourself if you have done these things. You now have the power to break free of the NBO so you can foster healthy relationship habits.

At your essence you are love.

If you have ever lived according to this myth, here are some of the lies that you are operating under:

- Your safety is dependent upon what other people do.
- In order to be safe, you have to get other people to act according to the demands of NBO.
- Controlling other people will help you get what you want.
- The people in your life cannot be trusted to make good choices.

The truth of the matter looks more like this:

- You are responsible for your well-being, and it is not dependent upon the actions of others.
- Getting others to buy into NBO's lies is the worst thing you can do.
- Attempting to control other people will only make matters worse.
- If you cannot trust the people you are in relationships with to make good choices, you need to reconsider your relationships.
- If your well-being depends on other people doing what you want, you will be constantly frustrated in life.

You are likely acting on this myth because you have passed control of your life on to NBO, and are trying to reclaim it by instead controlling other people and events. Instead, reclaim your own life!

NBO Myth #5: If I am in enough pain, I will get what I need from my relationships.

Many people with NBO engage in self-destructive behavior, including self-mutilation, starvation, binge eating, risky sexual relationships, and a host of addictive behaviors in a futile attempt to get their needs met. These self-destructive actions are an attempt to get the love that you need and deserve. Part of you wants others to see how much pain you are in, hoping that someone will come along and help. NBO thrives on this despair and dissatisfaction.

NBO is a signal that you are in need of help. There is nothing wrong with needing help! There's nothing to feel ashamed or embarrassed about. All human beings have needs and we all go through difficult times. NBO is a clear signal that you are in need, and you should listen to this information. The earlier you can identify NBO, the easier it will be to take back control of your life.

Here are some of the lies that you should be on the lookout for:

- You can get what you need by acting out of desperation.
- You deserve to live a life of pain and suffering.
- You are a victim of your circumstances.
- People should know what you need and be able to give it to you without you communicating it to them.
- You are unable to take care of yourself and need someone else to do it for you.

These lies need to be identified and torn out by their roots. The truth is:

- The anguish you feel is not about how you look; it is about self-worth and self-acceptance.
- The more clearly you voice your needs, the greater your chance of having them met.
- You deserve to live a life of abundance, joy, love, and success.

- Believing that you are a victim will never bring you lasting happiness.
- People can never know what you need if you do not communicate your feelings, nor can you know what other people need without them telling you.
- NBO thrives on the belief that you are unable to take care of yourself. You need to constantly affirm to yourself that you can and will care for yourself with the love and compassion that you deserve.

The lesson here is to ask for help clearly. You've already taken a big step by reading this book!

NBO Myth #6: I need to look different and be perfect in order to please my partner.

NBO develops in part because of our willingness to participate in destructive cultural norms, especially the belief that beauty means looking like a two-dimensional photo of a model. When we accept and internalize this value system, we put ourselves and our bodies at risk.

An extension of this socially induced hallucination is the belief that you need to be thin in order to please your partner. This may be a difficult myth to puncture because your partner may, in fact, have opinions about what your body should look like and how much you should weigh. (Neither men nor women are immune to the effects of social conditioning.) Or, your partner may love you regardless of your size or shape, but you still are unable to see yourself as worthwhile and desirable. In either case, understand that what your partner thinks about your body cannot be the sole determinant of your

The *only* perfection that exists is the perfection of *you* exactly as you are, *right here, right now,* in this *very moment.*

happiness. You must first and foremost cultivate a loving relationship with your own body.

Some lies that NBO uses to uphold Myth #6:

- What you see in magazines or on television is the only standard for being attractive.
- If you are not perfect, your partner will no longer want to be with you.
- It is your job to please your partner.
- Your self-worth and your desirability depend on what your partner thinks about your body.
- If you let yourself be who you truly are, your partner will not love you.

The truth sounds more like this:

- Beauty comes in all different shapes, sizes, and forms. You can break free from NBO and learn to see the beauty in diversity.
- The only perfection that exists is the perfection of you exactly as you are, right here, right now, in this very moment.
- If your partner only wants to be with you because of your body size, you need to find a new partner.
- It is your job to take care of yourself. Once you learn to love yourself and are comfortable in your own skin, you will attract the relationships you want into your life.
- Your self-worth and desirability depend on what you think and how you feel about yourself. Other people can influence your beliefs about yourself only if you let them.
- If your partner will not love you for who you truly are, then you need to take the risk of finding another partner who will cherish you as you are right now.

If you are lucky enough to have a supportive partner who loves you as you are, remember how the universe gives you what you need, when you need it. Perhaps this person is in your life not only to bring you love and joy, but also to help you overcome your struggle with NBO. On the other hand, if you need to end the relationship with your current partner, know that your awareness of who you are and what you need in a relationship will help you find someone who's right for you.

NBO Myth #7: I need to be perfect in order to please my family.

Although NBO sufferers are often accused of being selfish (see Myth #8), the opposite is generally the case: they are driven by a need to please and be approved of by other people. Many NBO sufferers are trying to please their parents and are literally or figuratively killing themselves in the process.

Some of the lies that NBO creates in this scenario include:

- My body is an indicator of my success as a family member.
- My family will love me more if I am perfect.
- My parents' issues are my issues.
- My family will be embarrassed by me if I don't have the perfect body.
- I can't live with the negative feelings my family might have about me.

The truth is:

- Your body size is not an indicator of your success or failure.
- If the love in your relationships is dependent on how you look, you must begin to rework your relationships so that they reflect your heart and soul instead of your body.

- Your parents' issues and challenges are not yours. As children we are influenced profoundly by our parents and their challenges, but as adults we must not unconsciously assume their struggles.
- Body image and health are topics that should be discussed and addressed with the whole family. The people who love you hopefully want you to make healthy choices, and you probably want them to do the same. Instead of worrying about how they perceive you, work together as a family to determine how to make healthier lifestyle choices for everyone.
- Our family ties have the deepest and strongest influence on our well-being because we have opened our hearts to these people. If your family relationships are marked by negative feelings, be willing to discuss them openly and honestly. It is only through successful communication that wounds can begin to heal and love can begin to flower.

This area may be one of particular angst for many of you. Don't be afraid to ask for help. Refer to the Break Free Beauty coaching and other resources in the Appendix, visit a therapist, or suggest that your entire family or certain members of your family attend a group session.

NBO Myth #8: I am selfish, unworthy, and incapable of meaningful relationships.

NBO can, in fact, make you look selfish because it completely monopolizes your attention, awareness, and focus. To the unaware and uninitiated, this can seem like the ultimate in self-centeredness and self-ishness. People who feel this way likely cannot see that you are actually a very giving and caring person; you are just giving everything you have to your relationship with NBO. Living with NBO is all-consuming and its lies are so seductive that you have probably prioritized that relationship over all the others in your life.

Some of the lies that NBO uses to uphold this myth are:

- You are too focused on yourself and never think of anyone else.
- You have a limited capacity for love.
- You are incapable of giving love and affection.
- You don't deserve love.

The facts of the matter might look something more like this:

- It is difficult, if not impossible, to focus on someone else when you are putting all of your attention into maintaining a relationship with NBO.
- You have a limitless capacity for love; you only need to heal your broken heart.
- You are capable of giving limitless love and affection to others, but you must first learn how to give it to yourself.
- You are deserving of all the love in the world. At your essence you are love; it is the central aspect of your being.

Though people may be wrong in their assessment of you, know that their opinions are formed by both their own thought patterns and by the lies that NBO puts forth. Work to eradicate NBO and the lies will disappear and your true self will be more apparent to you and everyone around you.

Start with Yourself First

Remember, you must first cultivate a loving relationship with yourself, body, mind, and soul before finding a meaningful relationship with another person. The exercises in this book have been designed to help facilitate this process. As you create peace, love, and affection within yourself, you will be able to create these same relationships with other people. As you create meaningful relationships with other people, it will help bolster your ability to love and accept yourself. This takes courage and strength, but take advantage of the many helpful resources and tools available:

- Learn to meditate as a couple or a family.
- Work on improving your communication skills through counseling.
- Find a support group to help navigate the challenges of living with NBO.
- Become engaged in a cause or activity you feel passionately about. This may be a particular hobby, environmental or other activism, or spiritual growth. Reach out to your local community and see where you can give back.
- Don't be afraid to be human! Many NBO sufferers believe they need to be perfect in order to fit in. The fact is the most beautiful person is someone who radiates a simple, unaffected humanity.
- Above all, don't listen to NBO's lies about how you should isolate yourself.

If you are a parent it is imperative that you take the necessary steps to heal. Children are intensely affected by their parents' beliefs, thoughts, actions, and behaviors. If you are a parent struggling with NBO, you should:

- Seek professional help. Find a coach or a counselor whom you trust and talk to him or her about your struggles and how they might be affecting your child.
- Become the example you want to be for your children. Learn to love yourself so that you can be the example of how your children should love themselves.
- Encourage healthy lifestyle choices in your children, but do not focus on their weight or body size. Focus instead on the quality of character that they have and can develop.
- Encourage your children to help other people and model for them the importance of giving back to the community.

If you are a parent, the most important thing you can ever do is to model the type of person you want your child to become. Children unconsciously and constantly model the behaviors of their parents.

Making Difficult Decisions

If you find yourself in a relationship with someone who is not supportive of your body and who you are, it is imperative that you either change it into a supportive relationship or end it. Remind yourself: You are inherently valuable and worthwhile. If the people closest to you do not honor you for the beautiful being that you are, be clear about what you want, need, and deserve from relationships.

If you are in a supportive relationship, that is wonderful. Although a partner can never give you the ability to love and accept yourself if you do not feel that way toward yourself, a supportive partner can aid in the process of healing. Honor your partner and use the relationship as another tool in helping you heal. The exercises listed in this chapter will be valuable in facilitating the healing process, while increasing intimacy and connection in your relationships.

If you are single, however, it is very natural to feel lonely and desire a relationship. For many of us, food can be used as a substitute for comfort and love. Learn how to offer yourself the comfort and love you desire by using

It is your job to take care of *yourself*. Once you learn to *love* yourself and are *comfortable* in your own skin, you will *attract* the relationships you want into your life.

the techniques discussed in this book. As you learn to love yourself, you will begin to experience more love wherever you go, both in relationships as well as alone. Although you may still want a relationship, you don't have to be in one for you to be happy.

It is only when you learn to connect intimately with yourself that you can learn to connect intimately with another person. When you learn to love and accept yourself fully, you can learn to love and accept another person fully. If you are single and lonely, follow the steps in this book, and continue to treat yourself with love and respect. When the time is right, you will attract the relationship you desire.

Working with Others

The following exercises can be used to improve relationships between people when one or both people struggle with Negative Body Obsession. The exercises can be used both by parents and their children, or by couples involved in a relationship, or even by friends. (Only the last two exercises are specifically designed for couples.)

If your partner will not love you for who you *truly* are, then you need to *take the risk* of finding another partner who will *cherish* you, as you are *right now*.

If you feel nervous about approaching someone to do the exercise with you, try saying something like this to break the ice: "You may know that I struggle with some negative thoughts about my body and my life. I am committed to overcoming them, but I could use your help. Would you be willing to take a few moments to complete some exercises with me?"

Identify How NBO Is Affecting Your Relationship

We've talked a lot about how NBO can have serious consequences in relationships. The first step in negating its influence is to identify NBO's presence and its impact on your life and relationship. Sit down together and make a list of all the ways NBO is affecting your relationship. It is very important not to create blame! NBO is no one's fault and any blame or guilt will be counterproductive. The point of this exercise is simply to bring awareness to the situation.

This exercise should be done in a spirit of love and acceptance. There may be many negative emotions, with people feeling angry, hurt, and frustrated on all sides. Learn how to experience these emotions, communicate them when necessary, and then let them go so that everyone can move toward greater healing.

Set an Intention Together

It is important to have intentions for your relationships as well as for yourself. What type of environment do you want to create as a family, as a couple, or as a friend? What would you like to see happen? Set an intention for what you would like to create. You can also develop a vision for your relationship, as well as specific goals. What type of healing would you like to experience? What is your vision for the future? What needs to happen to move you in the direction of your vision? What specific goals could move you from where you are to where you want to be? Be clear about what you want to change and make sure that everyone is on board with the intention.

Note: You may need to explain what an intention is, so the person doing the exercise with you has some background of the concept.

Learn to Meditate Together

As you know by now, meditation is a powerful tool for improving every area of your life. Learning to meditate as a couple or a family can provide additional energy, support, and encouragement. If you are a parent, your children will be more likely to practice meditation when they see you doing it. For couples, it can provide additional relaxation and connection. Meditation will provide you with the energy and power to create the type of relationship you want.

When you meditate together, you derive benefit simply from being in each other's presence. You both sit with your eyes closed, silently repeating your mantra or whichever meditation technique you are using, as if you were meditating alone. You have the added benefit, however, of being with another person and sharing in the experience.

Alternatively, one person can lead the meditation, instructing the others to take a few deep, relaxing breathes before meditation, and then paying attention to the time so the other people don't need to think about it.

Mirror Talk with Your Partner

This can be a provocative exercise for anyone, especially someone struggling with NBO. In Step 3, you learned how to do this mirror exercise with yourself (see page 112). Now you can do the same exercise as a couple.

Stand in front of the mirror naked, or in sexy lingerie, and tell each other what you admire and appreciate about one another's bodies. If you feel safe, you can even share with one another areas that you are uncomfortable with and work together to change how you look at that part of your body. Your partner can then tell you what he or she thinks is sexy about this part of your body.

Your goal is to learn to see beauty in yourself and your partner. Doing this exercise can transform your inner critic into your inner admirer. It is perfectly okay if this feels uncomfortable and embarrassing at first; just be open to the experience and share whatever emotions and feeling come up. If you practice this exercise consistently, it can improve your closeness, intimacy, and even your sex life!

Intimate Touch

This exercise can naturally follow the mirror exercise. Since you probably still feel uncomfortable in your body and about your body, you might have a tendency to cringe or want to disappear when someone touches the parts of your body that you dislike. This exercise will help you open yourself up to receiving all the love and affection that your partner has to offer. It may be challenging at first, but the uncomfortable feelings are your teachers and can lead you where you need to go. If you practice this exercise regularly, you will be amazed by the love and affection that you are able to give and receive.

After you have completed the mirror exercise, embrace one another. Begin to caress your lover and let him (or her) caress you. When you begin to feel uncomfortable, force yourself to think about the part of your body that you want to hide from. Focus on what it does for your body and the job it performs for you on a daily basis, and tell it you're grateful. Then tell your partner of your insecurity, and then let him assure you that he loves this part of your body. Open yourself up to receiving the love and affection that you're being offered. You might continue to feel uncomfortable; that's okay. Just breathe gently and try to relax a little more. Every time you notice yourself feeling uncomfortable or self-conscious, simply breathe and see if you can relax and open just a little bit more.

Over time, you will feel yourself becoming more and more expansive as you take down the walls you have constructed. You will learn to let yourself just be, without pretending, knowing that you are perfectly beautiful and wonderful just the way you are.

Ways to Ensure That You Are Moving in the Right Direction

Like anything in life, overcoming NBO and building a strong relationship is a process. It might happen quickly or it might happen slowly. The key is to continue the process once you start it. As you work through the exercises in this chapter, keep these goals in mind:

- Maintain honest and open communication.
- Revisit your intentions, visions, and goals regularly.
- Acknowledge positive changes and improvements.
- Encourage one another constantly to live in a state of love and abundance.

You can even set regular meetings to continue to talk, dream, and practice new tools and techniques to catapult your life and your relationship to the next level. Learning to truly love and accept one another, with all of our gifts and our idiosyncrasies, is to be like the Source, loving everyone unconditionally as you are loved unconditionally.

Points to Remember

- Become aware of NBO's myths:

    NBO Myth #1: I must isolate myself from people because the only thing that matters is how I look.
    NBO Myth #2: I need someone else to make me feel beautiful, safe, and good about myself.
    NBO Myth #3: I can have a successful relationship with a significant other even if I have NBO.
    NBO Myth #4: If I can fully control someone else, I will be safe.

NBO Myth #5: If I am in enough pain, I will get what I need from my relationships.

NBO Myth #6: I need to look different and be perfect in order to please my partner.

NBO Myth #7: I need to be perfect in order to please my family.

NBO Myth #8: I am selfish, unworthy of, and incapable of meaningful relationships.

- Realize that NBO can interfere with your ability to experience open, loving, and nurturing relationships.
- Affirm the truths in this chapter to debunk the myths and break free from NBO.
- Remember that loving yourself unconditionally is a prerequisite to creating loving relationships.
- Use the following exercises to improve your existing relationships.

  - Identify and discuss how NBO is affecting your relationship.
  - Set an intention together.
  - Learn to meditate together.
  - Do the mirror exercise.
  - Perform the intimate touch exercise.

CHAPTER TWELVE

Nurturing from Within

As you progress on this path of healing, it is very natural to experience challenges. You might feel as if you have relapsed, or fallen back. Your ego might even try to convince you that you have failed. In reality, however, you can never fail. You might go through periods of forgetfulness, where you lapse back into old patterns, beliefs, and behaviors, but this is just a momentary lapse in memory. Think of it as temporary amnesia. Previous patterns might re-emerge and reassert themselves, but your inherent beauty and your spiritual wisdom are always right there, underneath and beyond NBO with its negative conditioning. When you find yourself lapsing back into old ways of being, realize that you are simply in a forgetful moment. When you remember once again, you will continue on your way to creating all the joy, peace, love, and abundance you desire.

It's Okay to Relapse

NBO is a habit. For most, it is a lifelong habit. So if you find yourself being seduced by NBO, believing once again that you need to be thin in order to be lovable, or you start listening to Negative Body Thoughts, realize this is normal. It is simply a natural part of the process. Remind yourself that complete freedom from NBO is possible and achievable. Repeat this fact whenever you find yourself feeling as if you have relapsed.

Here are some practical suggestions for those times when you find yourself once again listening to NBO.

Review Your Intentions

Have you been reviewing your intentions regularly? You know very well by now that what you focus on with your mind, you begin to create in your life. Make sure that you are reviewing your intentions on a consistent basis. Read through your intentions before you go into meditation and before you go to bed. No need to obsess about them; just review them regularly to remind yourself of what you want to create.

Continually reviewing and affirming the intention to feel great in and about your body will gradually eclipse less productive intentions, such as "being as thin as possible" or "losing weight no matter what." Look for signs that your intentions are becoming reality. Whenever anything occurs that is in keeping with your intention, no matter how big or small, take time to acknowledge it. Acknowledging the progressive realization of your intentions will aid in their fulfillment. Also realize that you have all the time in the world. It is easy to create a tremendous amount of stress by worrying that you are not progressing quickly enough. Commit to your intentions, commit to practicing what you have learned in this book. Then trust that the process will take you where you need to go in the right amount of time.

Talk Back to Your Negative Body Thoughts!

Even after completing all of the exercises in Step 2, you might find those Negative Body Thoughts still hanging around in your head. The techniques you have learned will stay in your back pocket so you can pull them out any time you need to disengage. Over time, detaching from Negative Body Thoughts will become second nature. It will become a habit until you no longer need it at all.

Stay Aware

The first step is to fine-tune your awareness. As you know by now, change always begins with awareness. Be vigilant and notice whenever there is the slightest inkling of a Negative Body Thought. Sometimes your feelings will be your first alert that something is amiss. You may find that you start feeling sad, depressed, anxious, embarrassed, overwhelmed, hopeless, irritated, annoyed, or angry. You might sigh in resignation or burst into tears. Whenever you find yourself experiencing these negative emotions, stop and take a quick note of your thoughts.

> Review and affirm your intention to feel great *in* and *about* your body.

Have any Negative Body Thoughts infiltrated your awareness unannounced? Have they impeded your right to energy, abundance, and enlightenment? Are they disconnecting you from your source of all love and beauty? If so, it is time to disengage and get back on track.

Try talking back to your thoughts. You can tell Negative Body Thoughts "Get lost," "See you later," or "Leave me alone," or just say "Next." Make it clear that they are unwanted, unuseful, and unwelcome. Sometimes talking back is enough to send them packing!

Seek Outside Help

If your Negative Body Thoughts continue to harass you, there are many wonderful tools and techniques that have been developed to overcome negative thought patterns. As always, seek outside help and support when you need it. See the Resources section for a complete listing.

Develop a Physical Detachment Technique

Develop your own signature technique for detaching after becoming aware of a Negative Body Thought. It should be something physical that you can do anywhere to remind yourself that you don't need to listen to your current dialogue. You can flick your hand, shrug your shoulder, anything that feels right for you and that can be used on the go. Whenever you notice a Negative Body Thought, engage in this physical movement to remind yourself to detach from it. Then pick a replacement thought that affirms your beauty, goodness, and strength.

Keep Meditating!

Just as NBO is a habit, meditating is a habit. Make it part of your daily routine. Meditation is not something that you will start and then stop when you are feeling better. It is a lifelong journey that will yield profound returns over time.

If you have abandoned your meditation practice, recommit to making it part of your life. As you commit to practicing regularly, it will become like brushing your teeth. How often do you abandon the habit of brushing your teeth? Not often, I hope! Over time, your meditation practice will become a deeply rewarding, satisfying, and rejuvenating part of your life. If you feel that you simply cannot practice for thirty minutes twice a day, practice for however long you can. Something is always better than nothing, even if it is just for ten minutes! Review the practices in Step 3 to help you connect with your spiritual self. It is easy to forget when we are used to living without spirit. Take the time, especially in the beginning, to continually remind yourself of your true nature. Remember to always extend love and compassion to yourself.

Listen to Your Body

One of the hallmarks of NBO is that your body doesn't have a voice. NBO-sufferers have a history of always telling their bodies what to do and when. NBO has probably dictated what your body should look like, how it should function, how much it should exercise. After years of listening to NBO, it can be almost impossible to listen to your body. Even though your body might be screaming at the top of its lungs, it is still difficult for you to hear it underneath NBO's tyrannical commands.

Commit to fine-tuning your listening. Listening to the body is an art. Constantly notice what your body is wanting. Do you need to get more rest? Exercise less? Exercise more? You know by now that your body is truly brilliant, so fine-tune your listening capabilities. Your body will help lead you to greater healing and satisfaction. Realize also that your body's needs will change over time. You may find that what your body wanted two years ago is not what it wants today. Check in regularly to see what changes might need to be made.

Listen to Your Emotions

In life, sometimes listening is the most important skill. Cultivate your ability to listen to your heart, listen to your body, and listen to your soul. With practice, you will be amazed by how many answers you can get when you simply stop and listen. Learning to listen is really quite simple, although not always easy. Try this to get yourself started: Sit quietly with your eyes closed. Bring your attention to your body. You can ask yourself: "What am I really wanting?" Then simply wait and listen for a response. Don't get discouraged if you can't hear anything at first. With practice, it will become easier and easier to hear what you are truly wanting in each moment.

You are beautiful, lovable, and eminently worthwhile.

Revisit Your Peace Accord

Review the peace accord that you established between your body, mind, and spirit in Step 4. You might find yourself falling back into a war, with your intellect, emotions, and body arguing. When this happens, pull out the peace accord and make sure each side gets to be heard. Remember to have your spiritual self overseeing the process. This might sound silly, but it is very effective. We are often sabotaged by the competing voices within ourselves. Learn to dialogue with the different parts of yourself so that you can determine the healthiest and happiest way to move forward.

Here is an example to illustrate what I mean: Imagine you are busy at work and aren't getting as much sleep as you need. Every afternoon, your body craves sugar to keep working through the energy slump. Your mind starts reprimanding and getting angry at your body, scared that you might gain weight, and knowing that too much sugar is not healthy. Initiate a dialogue process between these different parts of yourself. Negotiate so that each side can get what it needs to help you move toward your dreams, goals, and aspirations.

Create a Purpose Ritual

Sometimes it can be difficult to know what your purpose is. Other times, you might know your purpose but feel that you can't live it because you are stuck in a dead-end job. When you feel stuck, as if you aren't quite living your purpose, it can be helpful to create a purpose ritual—something you do every day to embody and express your purpose wherever you are and whatever you are doing.

Here is an example. Let's say your purpose is to help bring joy into other people's lives. Come up with one ritual you could do each day to express this purpose. Is there someone you could call or e-mail to tell them how much you appreciate them? Could you take a couple of hours a week and volunteer at a home for the elderly or children? Could you write poetry and post it on a community blog? Get creative—it doesn't need to be anything grand, just a small ritual each day. This practice will help keep you on track with your purpose, solidifying against the negative influences of NBO. It will help you to overcome feeling that you can't live your purpose in

You are deserving of limitless compassion.

your current circumstances. It will help you begin to live your purpose wherever you are right now in your life.

Ask for Help

One final point: remember to get the help you need. NBO thrives on isolation. It often reappears in your life when you are faced with difficulties, whether relating to finance, relationships, or health. When a crisis hits, NBO often races to the rescue. If this happens, realize that it might be a signal to get help. Look at hiring a coach, joining a support group, talking to a therapist or even a friend—whatever it takes to get you the help you really need. NBO will never provide you with the solutions. Instead, get the support you need to process through your current challenges and create the life of your dreams. See the Resources section for referrals.

Remember Your Inherent Beauty

Realize and accept that absolutely wherever you are at is okay. If you find yourself forgetting, if you find yourself listening to NBO, offer yourself love, offer yourself understanding, offer yourself support. There is nothing wrong with you and no reason to be ashamed. When you feel frustrated and stuck, look for opportunities to bring more joy, more love, and more beauty into your life. As you begin to experience the bliss of your true self, NBO will eventually become a distant memory.

Remember that you are perfect exactly as you are; you are lovable exactly as you are, and you can create the joy you desire. This joy will not come from controlling your body, but from recognizing and experiencing your true brilliance and beauty.

Points to Remember

- Continuing to have occasional Negative Body Thoughts is simply a natural part of the process.
- Get in the habit of listening to your body.
- You are perfect exactly as you are, right now.
- Review your intentions regularly.
- Whenever you feel like you have relapsed, remind yourself that complete freedom from NBO is possible and achievable.
- Keep meditating!
- Create a purpose ritual.
- True bliss will come from recognizing and experiencing your true brilliance and beauty.

Conclusion

My intention with this book is that you experience the love, joy, peace, and abundance that is your birthright.

NBO thrives on isolation and insecurity. May this book serve as a source of connection, comfort, and love during any time of struggle. May it also help you pursue and achieve your dreams with passion, knowing that you can fulfill every desire you may have, now and in the future.

If you want extra help in overcoming Negative Body Obsession and creating a body and a life that you love, please visit my website, *www.sarahmaria.com*. I offer an individualized coaching program, seminars, retreats, and products designed to help you love your body and love your life. Become part of the community by signing up on the website— together, we will create a world where everyone recognizes his or her beauty and feels loved and cherished as unique, special, and ultimately divine all of the time.

May you experience boundless love every day of your life.

Peace, Love, Beauty,

Sarah Maria

Resources

Coaching

Break Free Beauty Coaching, Seminars, and Retreats
www.breakfreebeauty.com; www.sarahmaria.com
Receive individual, couple, and family assistance in learning to love
your body and your life.

Meditation Instruction

Primordial Sound Meditation
Break Free Beauty: *www.breakfreebeauty.com*
The Chopra Center: *www.chopra.com*
The Self-Centered Tour: *www.getselfcentered.com*

Mindfulness
Chodron, Prema. *Awakening Loving-Kindness.* (Shambhala, 1996)
Chodron, Prema. *Comfortable with Uncertainty: 108 Teachings.*
  (Shambhala, 2002)
Chodron, Prema. *No Time to Lose: A Timely Guide to the Way of the
  Bodhisattva.* (Shambhala, 2007)

Chodron, Prema. *The Places That Scare You: A Guide to Fearlessness in Difficult Times.* (Shambhala, 2007)

Chodron, Prema. *Practicing Peace in Times of War.* (Shambhala, 2007)

Chodron, Prema. *Start Where You Are: A Guide to Compassionate Living.* (Shambhala, 2004)

Chodron, Prema. *When Things Fall Apart: Heart Advice for Difficult Times.* (Shambhala, 2005)

Chodron, Prema. *The Wisdom of No Escape and the Path of Loving Kindness.* (Shambhala, 2001)

S. N. Goenka: *www.vri.dhamma.org*

Kornfeld, Jack. *After the Ecstasy, the Laundry: How the Heart Grows Wise on the Spiritual Path.* (Bantam, 1999)

Kornfeld, Jack. *Being Dharma: The Essence of the Buddha's Teachings.* (Shambhala, 2001)

Kornfeld, Jack. *A Path with Heart: A Guide Through the Perils and Promises of Spiritual Life.* (Bantam, 1993)

Kornfeld, Jack. *The Wise Heart: A Guide to the Universal Teachings of Buddhist Psychology.* (Bantam, 2008)

Sharon Salzberg: *www.sharonsalzberg.com*

Salzberg, Sharon. *Faith: Trusting Your Own Deepest Experience.* (Riverhead Trade, 2003)

Salzberg, Sharon. *Insight Meditation: A Step-by-Step Course on How to Meditate.* (Sounds True, 2002)

Salzberg, Sharon. *Lovingkindness: The Revolutionary Art of Happiness.* (Shambhala, 2008)

Spirit Rock: *www.spiritrock.org*

Zinn, Jon Kabat. *Arriving at Your Own Door: 108 Lessons in Mindfulness.* (Hyperion, 2007)

Zinn, Jon Kabat. *Coming to Our Senses: Healing Ourselves and the World Through Mindfulness.* (Hyperion, 2006)

Zinn, Jon Kabat. *Complementary and Alternative Medicine in Rehabilitation.* (Churchill Livingstone, 2002)

Zinn, Jon Kabat. *Everyday Blessings: The Inner Work of Mindful Parenting.* (Hyperion, 1998)

Zinn, Jon Kabat. *Full Catastrophe Living: Using the Wisdom of Your Body and Mind to Face Stress, Pain, and Illness.* (Delta, 1990)

Zinn, Jon Kabat. *Mindfulness Meditation for Everyday Life.* (Piatkus Books, 2001)

Zinn, Jon Kabat. *Wherever You Go, There You Are: Mindfulness Meditation in Everyday Life.* (Hyperion, 2005)

Ayurveda

The Ayurvedic Institute: *www.ayurveda.com*

The Chopra Center: *www.chopra.com*

Chopra, Deepak. *Perfect Health: The Complete Mind/Body Guide, Revised and Updated Edition.* (Harmony, 2001)

Dr. Vasant Lad: *www.ayurveda.com*

Lad, Vasant. *Ayurveda: The Science of Self-Healing.* (Lotus Press, 1984)

Lad, Vasant. *Ayurvedic Cooking for Self-Healing.* (Ayurvedic Press, 1997)

Lad, Vasant. *Ayurvedic Perspectives on Selected Pathologies: An Anthology of Essential Reading from Ayurveda Today.* (Ayurvedic Press, 2005)

Lad, Vasant. *The Complete Book of Ayurvedic Home Remedies.* (Three Rivers Press, 1999)

Lad, Vasant. *Marma Points of Ayurveda: The Energy Pathways for Healing Body, Mind, and Consciousness with a Comparison to Traditional Chinese Medicine.* (Ayurvedic Press, 2006)

Lad, Vasant. *Secrets of the Pulse: The Ancient Art of Ayurvedic Pulse Diagnosis.* (Ayurvedic Press, 1996)

Lad, Vasant. *Strands of Eternity.* (The Ayurvedic Press, 2006)

Lad, Vasant. *Textbook of Ayurveda, Volume One: Fundamental Principles.* (Ayurvedic Press, 2001)

Lad, Vasant. *Textbook of Ayurveda, Volume Two: A Complete Guide to Clinical Assessment.* (The Ayurvedic Press, 2007)

Lad, Vasant. *Yoga of Herbs, Ayurvedic Guide.* (Lotus Press, 2001)

Dr. David Frawley: *www.vedanet.com*

Frawley, David. *Astrology of the Seers.* (Lotus Press, 2000)

Frawley, David. *Ayurveda and Marma Therapy: Energy Points in Yogic Healing.* (Lotus Press, 2003)

Frawley, David. *Ayurveda and the Mind.* (Lotus Press, 1997)

Frawley, David. *Ayurvedic Astrology: Self-Healing Through the Stars.* (Lotus Press, 2005)

Frawley, David. *Ayurvedic Healing: A Comprehensive Guide.* (Lotus Press, 2000)

Frawley, David. *Gods, Sages and Kings.* (Lotus Press, 2000)

Frawley, David. *Inner Tantric Yoga: Working with the Universal Shakti: Secrets of Mantras, Deities, and Meditation.* (Lotus Press, 2009)

Frawley, David. *Neti: Healing Secrets of Yoga and Ayurveda.* (Lotus Press, 2005)

Frawley, David. *Planetary Herbology: An Integration of Western Herbs into the Traditional Chinese and Ayurvedic Systems.* (New Delhi: Motilal Banarsidass, 2003)

Frawley, David. *The Rig Veda.* (New Delhi: Aditya Prakashan, 2003)

Frawley, David. *Tantric Yoga and the Wisdom Goddesses.* (Lotus Press, 1994)

Frawley, David. *Vedantic Meditation: Lighting the Flame of Awareness.* (North Atlantic Books, 2000)

Frawley, David. *Wisdom of the Ancient Seers.* (Lotus Press, 1992)

Frawley, David. *Yoga and Ayurveda Book.* (Lotus Press, 1999)

Frawley, David. *Yoga for Your Type.* (Lotus Press, 2001)

Frawley, David. *Yoga of Herbs, Ayurvedic Guide, Second Revised and Enlarged Edition.* (Lotus Press, 2001)

Frawley, David. *Yoga: The Greater Tradition (Mandala Wisdom 4).* (Mandala Publishing, 2008)

Spirituality

Deepak Chopra: *www.deepakchopra.com; www.chopra.com*

Chopra, Deepak. *The Afterlife Experiments: Breakthrough Scientific Evidence of Life After Death.* (Atria, 2003)

Chopra, Deepak. *The Book of Secrets: Unlocking the Hidden Dimensions of Your Life.* (Three Rivers Press, 2005)

Chopra, Deepak. *Buddha: A Story of Enlightenment.* (HarperOne, 2008)

Chopra, Deepak. *The Chopra Center Cookbook: A Nutritional Guide to Renewal/Nourishing Body and Soul.* (Wiley, 2003)

Chopra, Deepak. *Contact: The Yoga of Relationship.* (Insight Editions, 2006)

Chopra, Deepak. *The Essential How to Know God: The Essence of the Soul's Journey into the Mystery of Mysteries.* (Harmony, 2007)

Chopra, Deepak. *The Essential Spontaneous Fulfillment of Desire: The Essence of Harnessing the Infinite Power of Coincidence.* (Harmony, 2007)

Chopra, Deepak. *Fire in the Heart: A Spiritual Guide for Teens.* (Simon Pulse, 2006)

Chopra, Deepak. *Freedom from Addiction: The Chopra Center Method for Overcoming Destructive Habits.* (HCI, 2007)

Chopra, Deepak. *Golf for Enlightenment: The Seven Lessons for the Game of Life.* (Rider & Co, 2005)

Chopra, Deepak. *How to Know God.* (Running Press Miniature Editions, 2001)

Chopra, Deepak. *Jesus: A Story of Enlightenment.* (HarperOne, 2008)

Chopra, Deepak. *Kama Sutra.* (Virgin Books, 2007)

Chopra, Deepak. *Life after Death: The Burden of Proof.* (Three Rivers Press, 2008)

Chopra, Deepak. *Magical Beginnings, Enchanted Lives.* (Three Rivers Press, 2005)

Chopra, Deepak. *Peace Is the Way: Bringing War and Violence to an End.* (Harmony, 2005)

Chopra, Deepak. *Power, Freedom and Grace: Living from the Source of Lasting Happiness.* (Amber-Allen Publishing, 2008)

Chopra, Deepak. *The Seven Spiritual Laws for Parents: Guiding Your Children to Success and Fulfillment.* (Three Rivers Press, 2006)

Chopra, Deepak. *The Seven Spiritual Laws of Success: A Pocketbook Guide to Fulfilling Your Dreams (One Hour of Wisdom).* (Amber-Allen Publishing, 2007)

Chopra, Deepak. *Soulmate: A Novel of Eternal Love.* (Signet, 2004)

Chopra, Deepak. *The Spontaneous Fulfillment of Desire: Harnessing the Infinite Power of Coincidence.* (Random House, 2003)

Chopra, Deepak. *Synchrodestiny.* (Rider & Co, 2005)

Chopra, Deepak. *The Ten Commitments: Translating Good Intentions into Great Choices.* (HCI, 2006)

Chopra, Deepak. *The Third Jesus: The Christ We Cannot Ignore.* (Harmony, 2008)

Chopra, Deepak. *Why Is God Laughing? The Path to Joy and Spiritual Optimism.* (Harmony, 2008)

Wayne Dyer: *www.drwaynedyer.com; www.hayhouse.com*

Dyer, Wayne. *A Promise Is a Promise.* (Hay House, 2001)

Dyer, Wayne. *Being in Balance.* (Hay House, 2006)

Dyer, Wayne. *Change Your Thoughts—Change Your Life: Living the Wisdom of the Tao.* (Hay House, 2007)

Dyer, Wayne. *Choosing Your Own Greatness.* (Your Coach in a Box, 2005)

Dyer, Wayne. *Creating Your World the Way You Really Want It to Be.* (Hay House, 2002)

Dyer, Wayne. *Getting in the Gap: Making Conscious Contact with God Through Meditation.* (Hay House, 2004)

Dyer, Wayne. *Gifts from Eykis: A Story of Self-Discovery.* (Quill, 2002)

Dyer, Wayne. *Inspiration: Your Ultimate Calling.* (Hay House, 2007)

Dyer, Wayne. *The Invisible Force: 365 Ways to Apply the Power of Intention to Your Life.* (Hay House, 2007)

Dyer, Wayne. *It's Not What You've Got.* (Hay House, 2007)

Dyer, Wayne. *Living the Wisdom of the Tao: The Complete Tao Te Ching and Affirmations.* (Hay House, 2008)

Dyer, Wayne. *The Power of Intention.* (Hay House, 2005)

Dyer, Wayne. *Real Magic: Creating Miracles in Everyday Life.* (Harper Paperbacks, 2001)

Dyer, Wayne. *Secrets of Your Own Healing Power.* (Hay House, 2005)

Dyer, Wayne. *10 Secrets for Success and Inner Peace.* (Hay House, 2002)

Dyer, Wayne. *There's a Spiritual Solution to Every Problem.* (Harper Paperbacks, 2003)

Dyer, Wayne. *What Do You Really Want for Your Children?* (Harper Paperbacks, 2001)

Dyer, Wayne. *Wisdom of the Ages: 60 Days to Enlightenment.* (Harper Collins, 1998)

Dyer, Wayne. *Your Erroneous Zones.* (Avon Books, 1993)

Dyer, Wayne. *Your Ultimate Calling: 365 Ways to Bring Inspiration into Your Life.* (Hay House, 2008)

Hawkins, R. David. *Power vs. Force.* (Hay House, 2002)

Maharaj, Sri Nisargadatta. *I Am That: Talks with Sri Nisargadatta Maharaj.* (Acorn Press, 1990)

Eckhart Tolle: *www.eckharttolle.com*

Tolle, Eckhart. *The Diamond in Your Pocket: Discovering Your True Radiance.* (Sounds True, 2007)

Tolle, Eckhart. *Milton's Secret: An Adventure of Discovery Through Then, When, and the Power of Now.* (Hampton Roads, 2008)

Tolle, Eckhart. *A New Earth: Awakening to Your Life's Purpose.* (Penguin, 2008)

Tolle, Eckhart. *A New Earth Inspiration Deck.* (New World Library, 2008)

Tolle, Eckhart. *Oneness with All Life: Inspirational Selections from a New Earth.* (Dutton Adult, 2008)

Tolle, Eckhart. *Practicing the Power of Now: Essential Teachings, Meditations, and Exercises from the Power of Now.* (New World Library, 2001)

Tolle, Eckhart. *Stillness Speaks.* (New World Library, 2003)

Venkatesananda, Swami. *Concise Yoga Vasistha.* (State University of New York Press, 1984)

Hay House: publishing company offering a wide-range of spiritual resources—*www.hayhouse.com*

Scientific Studies in Intention and Non-locality

Institute of Noetic Sciences: *www.noetic.org*

Lynn McTaggart: *http://livingthefield.ning.com*

McTaggart, Lynn. *The Field: The Quest for the Secret Force of the Universe.* (Harper Collins Canada, 2002)

McTaggart, Lynn. *The Intention Experiment: Using Your Thoughts to Change Your Life and the World.* (Harper Collins Canada, 2006)

Dean Radin: *www.deanradin.com*

Radin, Dean. *The Conscious Universe: The Scientific Truth of Psychic Phenomena.* (HarperOne, 1997)

Radin, Dean. *Entangled Minds: Extrasensory Experiences in a Quantum Reality.* (Paraview Pocket Books, 2006)

Russell Targ: *www.espresearch.com*

Targ, Russell. *Development of Techniques to Enhance Man/Machine Communication.* (Stanford Research Institute, 1974)

Targ, Russell. *Do You See What I See? Memoirs of a Blind Biker.* (Hampton Roads, 2008)

Targ, Russell. *End of Suffering: Fearless Living in Troubled Times.* (Hampton Roads, 2006)

Targ, Russell. *Limitless Mind: A Guide to Remote Viewing and Transformation of Consciousness.* (New World Library, 2004)

Targ, Russell. *The Mind Race Understanding and Using Psychic Abilities.* (Ballantine Books, 1985)

Targ, Russell. *Mind-Reach: Scientists Look at Psychic Ability.* (Hampton Roads, 2005)

Success and Achievement

Jack Canfield: *www.jackcanfield.com*

Canfield, Jack. *The Success Principles: How to Get from Where You Are to Where You Want to Be.* (Harper Collins, 2005)

Brian Tracy: numerous audio programs, *www.briantracy.com*

Health and Fitness

Bob Greene: *www.thebestlife.com*

Greene, Bob. *The Best Life Diet.* (Simon & Schuster, 2007)

Greene, Bob. *The Best Life Diet Cookbook: More than 100 Delicious, Convenient, Family-Friendly Recipes.* (Simon & Schuster, 2008)

Greene, Bob. *The Best Life Diet Daily Journal.* (Simon & Schuster, 2006)

Greene, Bob. *Get with the Program!: Getting Real about Your Weight, Health, and Emotional Well-Being.* (Simon & Schuster, 2003)

Greene, Bob. *The Get with the Program! Guide to Fast Food and Family Restaurants.* (Simon & Schuster, 2003)

Greene, Bob. *The Get with the Program! Guide to Good Eating: Great Food for Good Health.* (Simon & Schuster, 2002)

Greene, Bob. *Keep the Connection: Choices for a Better Body and a Healthier Life.* (Hyperion, 2003)

Greene, Bob. *Make the Connection: Ten Steps to a Better Body and a Better Life* (Hyperion, 1999)

Greene, Bob. *Total Body Makeover.* (Simon & Schuster, 2004)

Dr. Dean Ornish: *www.ornishspectrum.com*

Ornish, Dean. *Spectrum: A Scientifically Proven Program to Feel Better, Live Longer, Lose Weight, and Gain Health.* (Ballantine Books, 2007)

Bill Phillips: *www.bodyforlife.com*

Phillips, Bill. *Body for Life.* (Harper Collins, 1999)

Shawn Phillips: *www.mystrengthforlife.com*

Phillips, Shawn. *Strength for Life: The Fitness Plan for the Rest of Your Life.* (Ballantine Books, 2008)

Dr. Michael Roizen and Mehmet Oz: *www.realage.com*

Roizen, Michael and Mehmet Oz. *You on a Diet: The Owner's Manual for Waist Management.* (Free Press, 2006)

Overcoming Negative Thought Patterns/ Brain Health/Personal Growth

Dr. Daniel Amen: *www.brainplace.com*

Amen, Daniel. *ADD in Intimate Relationships: A Comprehensive Guide for Couples.* (Mindworks Press, 2005)

Amen, Daniel. *Change Your Brain, Change Your Life: The Breakthrough Program for Conquering Anxiety, Depression, Obsessiveness, Anger, and Impulsiveness.* (Three Rivers Press, 1999)

Amen, Daniel. *Clinician's Brain Science Toolbox.* (Mindworks Press, 2004)

Amen, Daniel. *Don't Shoot Yourself in the Foot.* (Grand Central Publishing, 1992)

Amen, Daniel. *The Healing ADD Power Program.* (Mindworks Press, 2005)

Amen, Daniel. *Healing ADD: The Breakthrough Program That Allows You to See and Heal the 6 Types of ADD.* (Berkley Books, 2001)

Amen, Daniel. *Healing Anxiety and Depression.* (Berkley Trade, 2004)

Amen, Daniel. *Healing the Hardware of the Soul: Enhance Your Brain to Improve Your Work, Love, and Spiritual Life.* (Free Press, 2008)

Amen, Daniel. *How to Get Out of Your Way: A Step-by-Step Guide for Identifying and Achieving Your Goals.* (Mindworks Press, 2005)

Amen, Daniel. *Images into the Mind: A Radical New Look at Understanding and Changing Behavior.* (Mindworks Press, 1995)

Amen, Daniel. *Magnificent Mind at Any Age: Natural Ways to Unleash Your Brain's Maximum Potential.* (Harmony, 2008)

Amen, Daniel. *Making a Good Brain Great: The Amen Clinic Program for Achieving and Sustaining Optimal Mental Performance.* (Harmony, 2005)

Amen, Daniel. *Mind Coach: How to Teach Children and Teenagers to Think Positive and Feel Good.* (Mindworks Press, 1997)

Amen, Daniel. *New Skills for Frazzled Parents: The Instruction Manual That Should Have Come with Your Child.* (Mindworks Press, 2000)

Amen, Daniel. *Preventing Alzheimer's: Ways to Help Prevent, Delay, Detect, and Even Halt Alzheimer's Disease and Other Forms of Memory Loss.* (Perigee Trade, 2005)

Amen, Daniel. *The Secrets of Successful Students.* (Mindworks Press, 2005)

Amen, Daniel. *Sex on the Brain: 12 Lessons to Enhance Your Love Life.* (Three Rivers Press, 2008)

Amen, Daniel. *Two Minutes a Day to a Lifetime of Love.* (St. Martin's Press, 1996)

Amen, Daniel. *What I Learned from a Penguin: A Story on How to Help People Change.* (Mindworks Press, 2005)

Hale Dwoskin, Sedona Method: *www.sedona.com*

Dwoskin, Hale. *Freedom Now: Your Key to Lasting Happiness, Abundance and Well-being.* (Sedona Press, 2003)

Dwoskin, Hale. *Happiness Is Free: And It's Easier than You Think!* (Sedona Training Associates, 2001)

Dwoskin, Hale. *The Sedona Method Course, Vols. 1–2.* (Sedona Trinity Associates, 2001)

Dwoskin, Hale. *The Sedona Method: Your Key to Lasting Happiness, Success, Peace and Emotional Well-Being.* (Sedona Press, 2003)

Daniel Goleman: *www.danielgoleman.info*

Goleman, Daniel. *Building Emotional Intelligence: Techniques to Cultivate Inner Strength in Children.* (Sounds True, 2008)

Goleman, Daniel. *The Creative Spirit.* (Plume, 1993)

Goleman, Daniel. *Destructive Emotions: A Scientific Dialogue with the Dalai Lama.* (Bantam, 2004)

Goleman, Daniel. *Emotional Intelligence: Why It Can Matter More than IQ.* (Bantam, 2006)

Goleman, Daniel. *The Emotionally Intelligent Workplace: How to Select for, Measure, and Improve Emotional Intelligence in Individuals, Groups, and Organizations.* (Jossey-Bass, 2001)

Goleman, Daniel. *Harvard Business Review on Breakthrough Leadership.* (Harvard Business School Press, 2002)

Goleman, Daniel. *Harvard Business Review on What Makes a Leader.* (Harvard Business School Press, 2001)

Goleman, Daniel. *Healing Emotions: Conversations with the Dalai Lama on Mindfulness, Emotions, and Health.* (Shambhala, 2003)

Goleman, Daniel. *Measuring the Immeasurable: The Scientific Case for Spirituality.* (Sounds True, 2008)

Goleman, Daniel. *The Meditative Mind.* (Tarcher, 1996)

Goleman, Daniel. *Mind Body Medicine: How to Use Your Mind for Better Health.* (Consumer Reports Books, 1995)

Goleman, Daniel. *The New Leaders.* (Time Warner Paperbacks, 2003)

Goleman, Daniel. *Primal Leadership: Learning to Lead with Emotional Intelligence.* (Harvard Business School Press, 2004)

Goleman, Daniel. *Raising an Emotionally Intelligent Child.* (Simon & Schuster, 1998)

Goleman, Daniel. *Social Intelligence: The New Science of Human Relationships.* (Bantam, 2007)

Goleman, Daniel. *Transparency: How Leaders Create a Culture of Candor.* (Jossey-Bass, 2008)

Goleman, Daniel. *Vital Lies, Simple Truths: The Psychology of Self-Deception.* (Simon & Schuster, 1996)

Goleman, Daniel. *Working with Emotional Intelligence.* (Bantam, 2000)

Goleman, Daniel. *Working with Presence: A Leading with Emotional Intelligence Conversation with Peter Senge.* (Macmillan Audio, 2006)

Hoffman Process: *www.hoffmaninstitute.org*

Byron Katie: *www.thework.com*

Katie, Byron. *Loving What Is: Four Questions That Can Change Your Life.* (Three Rivers Press, 2003)

Katie, Byron. *Question Your Thinking, Change the World: Quotations from Byron Katie.* (Hay House, 2007)

Katie, Byron. *Who Would You Be Without Your Story?: Dialogues with Byron Katie.* (Hay House, 2008)

Shimoff, Marci. *Happy for No Reason: 7 Steps to Being Happy from the Inside Out.* (Free Press, 2008)

Medical

Herbert Benson: *www.mbmi.com*

Benson, Herbert. *Beyond the Relaxation Response: How to Harness the Healing Power of Your Personal Beliefs.* (Berkley, 1994)

Benson, Herbert. *The Breakout Principle: How to Activate the Natural Trigger That Maximizes Creativity, Athletic Performance, Productivity and Personal Well-Being.* (Scribner, 2003)

Benson, Herbert. *Harvard Medical School Guide to Lowering Your Blood Pressure.* (McGraw-Hill, 2005)

Benson, Herbert. *How to Activate the Breakout Principle.* (Simon & Schuster, 1995)

Benson, Herbert. *The Mind/Body Effect.* (Berkley, 1980)

Benson, Herbert. *The Science of Sciences.* (Chinmaya Publications, 2006)

Benson, Herbert. *Stress Management: Techniques for Preventing and Treating Stress.* (Harvard Medical School, 2008)

Benson, Herbert. *Timeless Healing—The Power and Biology of Belief.* (Scribner, 1996)

Benson, Herbert. *Wellness Book: The Comprehensive Guide to Maintaining Health and Treating Stress-Related Illness.* (Scribner, 1993)

Larry Dossey: *www.dosseydossey.com*

Dossey, Larry. *Beyond Illness.* (Shambhala, 1985)

Dossey, Larry. *Coyote Healing: Miracles in Native Medicine.* (Bear & Company, 2003)

Dossey, Larry. *The Energy of Prayer: How to Deepen Your Spiritual Practice.* (Parallax Press, 2006)

Dossey, Larry. *The Extraordinary Healing Power of Ordinary Things: Fourteen Natural Steps to Health and Happiness.* (Three Rivers Press, 2007)

Dossey, Larry. *Healing Beyond the Body: Medicine and the Infinite Reach of the Mind.* (Shambhala, 2003)

Dossey, Larry. *Healing Breakthroughs.* (Piatkus Books, 1993)

Dossey, Larry. *Healing Through Prayer: Health Practitioners Tell the Story.* (Dundurn Press, 1999)

Dossey, Larry. *Healing Words.* (HarperOne, 1997)

Dossey, Larry. *Meaning and Medicine.* (Bantam Books, 1997)

Dossey, Larry. *The Mystery of Light: The Life and Teaching of Omraam Mikhael Aivanhov.* (Integral Publishing, 1998)

Dossey, Larry. *Prayer Is Good Medicine: How to Reap the Healing Benefits of Prayer.* (HarperOne, 1997)

Dossey, Larry. *Prayers for Healing: 365 Blessings, Poems, and Meditations from Around the World.* (Conari Press, 1997)

Dossey, Larry. *Recovering the Soul: A Scientific and Spiritual Approach.* (Bantam, 1989)

Dossey, Larry. *Reinventing Medicine: Beyond Mind-Body to a New Era of Healing.* (HarperOne, 2000)

Dossey, Larry. *Space, Time and Medicine.* (Shambhala, 1982)

Dossey, Larry. *Transformers: The Artists of Self-Creation.* (DeVorss & Co., 1994)

Dossey, Larry. *The Way of Qigong: The Art and Science of Chinese Energy Healing* (Wellspring/Ballantine, 1999)

Bruce Lipton: The Biology of Belief—*www.brucelipton.com*

Lipton, Bruce. *The Biology of Belief: Unleashing the Power of Consciousness, Matter and Miracles.* (Mountain of Love, 2005)

Lipton, Bruce. *Spontaneous Evolution: Our Positive Future and How to Get There from Here.* (Sounds True, 2008)

Lipton, Bruce. *The Wisdom of Your Cells: How Your Beliefs Control Your Biology.* (Sounds True, 2006)

Candace Pert: Molecules of Emotion—*www.candacepert.com*

Pert, Candace. *Everything You Need to Know to Feel Good.* (Hay House, 2007)

Pert, Candace. *Feel Happy Now!* (Hay House, 2008)

Pert, Candace. *Molecules of Emotion: The Science Behind Mind-Body Medicine.* (Scribner, 1997)

Pert, Candace. *Potatoes Not Prozac: A Natural Seven-Step Dietary Plan to Stabilize the Level of Sugar in Your Blood, Control Your Cravings and Lose Weight.* (Simon & Schuster, 1999)

Pert, Candace. *Smart Moves: Why Learning Is Not All in Your Head.* (Great Ocean Publishers, 2005)

Dr. David Simon: *www.chopra.com*

Simon, David. *The Chopra Center Herbal Handbook: Forty Natural Prescriptions for Perfect Health.* (Three Rivers Press, 2000)

Simon, David. *Free to Love, Free to Heal: Heal Your Body by Healing Your Emotions.* (Chopra Center Press, 2009)

Simon, David. *Return to Wholeness: Embracing Body, Mind, and Spirit in the Face of Cancer.* (Wiley, 1999)

Simon, David. *The Seven Spiritual Laws of Yoga: A Practical Guide to Healing Body, Mind, and Spirit.* (Wiley, 2004)

Simon, David. *The Ten Commitments: Translating Good Intentions into Great Choices.* (HCI, 2006)

Simon, David. *Vital Energy: The 7 Keys to Invigorate Body, Mind, and Soul.* (Wiley, 1999)

Bibliography

Anderson, Judith L. "Was the Duchess of Windsor Right? A Cross-Cultural Review of the Sociology of Ideals of Female Body Shape." *Ethology and Sociobiology* 13 (1992): 197–227.

Barber, Nigel. "Secular Changes in Standards of Bodily Attractiveness in American Women: Different Masculine and Feminine Ideals." *Journal of Psychology* 132(1) (1998): 87–94.

Benson, Herbert, MD. *Timeless Healing*. New York: Simon and Schuster, 1996.

Braud, William G. "Distant Mental Influence of Rate of Hemolysis of Human Red Blood Cells." *Journal of the American Society for Psychical Research* 84(1) (1990): 1–24.

Byrd, Randolph C. "Positive Therapeutic Effects of Intercessory Prayer in a Coronary Care Unit Population." *Southern Medical Journal* 81(7) (1988): 826–29.

Grad, B. "Dimensions in 'Some Biological Effects of the Laying On of Hands' and Their Implications." In *Dimensions in Wholisitic Healing: New Frontiers in the Treatment of the Whole Person*, edited by H. A. Otto and J. W. Knight. Chicago: Nelson-Hall, 1979.

Grad, B. "Some Biological Effects of 'Laying On of Hands': A Review of Experiments with Animals and Plants." *Journal of the American Society for Psychical Research* 59 (1965): 95–127.

Haraldsson, E. and T. Thorsteinsson. "Psychokinetic Effects on Yeast: An Exploration Experiment." In *Research in Parapsychology 1972*, edited by W. E. Roll et al. Metuchen, NJ: Scarecrow Press, 1973.

Harris, W. et al. "A Randomized, Controlled Trial of the Effects of Remote, Intercessory Prayer on Outcomes in Patients Admitted to the Coronary Care Unit." *Archives of Internal Medicine* 159(19) (1999): 2273–78.

Mosely, J. B. et al. "A Controlled Trial of Arthoscopic Surgery for Osteoarthritis in the Knee." *New England Journal of Medicine* 347(2) (2002): 81–88.

Sicher, F. et al. "A Randomized, Double-Blind Study of the Effect of Distant Healing in a Population with Advanced AIDS: Report of a Small Scale Study." *Western Journal of Medicine* 168(6) (1998): 356–63.

About the Author

 Sarah Maria is a body-image expert who shows people how to love their bodies and their lives. Her mission is to empower people of all ages, races, and body sizes to embrace the bodies they have been given and learn to love themselves so they can live their dreams.

Her company, Break Free Beauty, offers individual coaching, seminars, retreats, a membership program, and numerous continuing education opportunities designed to help people create bodies and lives that they love. It also offers a coach certification program. The Break Free Beauty coaching program trains coaches in body-image improvement techniques. She teaches her signature five-step process for breaking free so that more people can learn how to love their bodies and their lives.

To learn more about individual coaching, seminars, retreats, membership, continuing education, and coach certification, please visit *www.breakfreebeauty.com*. You can also send an e-mail to *info@breakfreebeauty.com*.

Together we will create a beautiful world!

Index